Surviving to Thriving
How to Overcome Setbacks and Rock Your Life

Surviving to Thriving:
How to Overcome Setbacks and Rock Your Life

By
Sheryl Green

Copyright © 2018: Something to Chew On Publishing.

All rights reserved.

No portion of this book may be reproduced in any form or by any means without permission in writing from the publisher, except for the inclusion of brief quotations in a review.

Cover: Jessica Cline

Cover Photograph: Melanie Rose, Las Vegas Event Photos

ISBN - 978-1-7323311-3-6

Printed in the United States of America

Something to Chew On Publishing • Las Vegas

Dedication

To all of the wonderful people that have helped me in my darkest times, and all of the animals (including my baby, Akasha) that have bestowed upon me the honor of being their voice. I love you all. This book is dedicated to you.

"I believe in the good things comin', comin', comin', comin'"

- Nahko and Medicine for the People

Table of Contents

Introduction 3

Chapter 1 11
How Do I Use This Book?

Chapter 2 14
The Drowning Giraffe

Chapter 3 26
Charlotte's Web of Emotional Support

Chapter 4 32
Warning Signs, Wake Up Calls, and Wombats

Chapter 5 41
Be a Duck

Chapter 6 50
At Least I'm Not On Fire!

Chapter 7 57
Your life makes me feel better about mine.

Chapter 8 65
What's Your Cause?

Chapter 9 77
I'm Good Enough, I'm Smart Enough, and Gosh Darn It, People Like Me

Chapter 10 89
Grab Fear By the Balls or (The Diaper List)

Chapter 11 .... **105**
Who Do You *Really* Want To Be?

Chapter 12 .... **114**
Everything Sucks.....But Maybe?

Chapter 13 .... **123**
We Regret To Inform You That Your White Knight Is Pending Administrative Review

Chapter 14 .... **132**
The Platinum Rule

Chapter 15 .... **146**
You Should Do Stand-Up

Chapter 16 .... **153**
Poof! You Are Resilient

Chapter 17 .... **155**
If At First You Don't Succeed

"Sometimes you've gotta get through your fear to see the beauty on the other side."

- *The Good Dinosaur*

Acknowledgments

It's been said that you should write with the door closed and edit with it open. During the whole process, not only was my door open, but my room and my heart were filled with others. First, I want to thank my parents. I would not be where I am today if it were not for their encouragement, their support, and their help getting off the proverbial (and literal) floor during my hardest times. I love you so much.

I'd like to thank all of my friends who have helped me develop, write, and edit this book. My editor, Taryn Wittenwiler; Jessica Cline who keeps my ellipses addiction under control; Clayton Waldhalm who keeps my comma addiction under control and sends me videos of puppies when I'm freaking out; and Richard Warren who got me started on this path..

A big thank you to Kathi Kulesza who has become like a sister to me and who is always there to listen to my problems and then remind me to take my own advice.

At every step of this process (the book, the speaking, and the journey I am on), there have been mentors taking me to the next step. Thank you Richard Warren (yup, you get two mentions!), Guy Dawson, Darren LaCroix, George Gilbert, and everyone else who has taught me something along the way.

And last but not least, I want to thank my animal rescue family, both the two legged and the four legged. Kelly McMahon, you are my oldest friend in Las Vegas and one of the best human beings that I know. Thank you for showing me how much power a single voice can have. Christy Stevens, you not only rescue animals, you rescue people. Thank you for changing the course of my life.

Introduction

Shit happens.

It's true. No matter how good your life is, no matter how much you plan ahead and anticipate problems before they arise, shit happens. (If you haven't already gotten the idea, I've got a bit of a potty mouth. If that offends you, skip to the "How to Use this Book" section for some helpful tips.)

There is nothing you can do to change the fact that sometimes, bad things are going to happen. What you can change is how you react to the aforementioned shit. Whether you weather the storm, drown in the puddles, or build an ark and rescue the world — that is the only choice you get to make.

We are talking about resilience. What makes some people able to survive the rough patches, while other people end up broken and hollow?

In *Under the Tuscan Sun* (one of my favorite movies — nope I'm not ashamed at all), the best friend is talking to the main character after her divorce and says:

"I think you're in danger... of never recovering. You know when you come across one of those empty-shell people and you think 'What the hell happened to you?' Well there came a time in each one of those lives where they were standing at a crossroads... Some place where they had to decide to turn left or right. This is no time to be a chicken shit, Francis."

Let's put niceties aside for a moment and be honest. You've seen those people. They are at the grocery store, the doctor's office, waiting in line at the movies. You look over and think to yourself, "Geez, they've had it rough." I believe the term "ridden hard and put away wet" may be appropriate here. There is a good possibility that they haven't lived through anything worse than you or I, so what's the difference?

We'll get to that.

First, I want to talk a little bit about resilience. It's got two definitions according to Merriam-Webster:

1: The capability of a strained body to recover its size and shape after deformation caused especially by compressive stress;

2: An ability to recover from or adjust easily to misfortune or change.

People often refer to it as "bouncing back." I want to tell you why I think that term is bullshit. Bouncing back suggests that you started at point A (or the beginning of your character arc for you writerly types); experienced your shit storm (this is the conflict in a story); hit your climax (mind out of the gutter please, this means that you overcame your conflict); and ended up... IN THE SAME EXACT PLACE. Writer folks, that means that your character arc was more of a ray.

Now I ask you, why the hell would you want to do that? Why would you want to face trials and tribulations, only to become the same exact person you were before? That seems like a waste of a perfectly good period of suckage.

What's our other option? Faking our own death and starting over?

Nope. Not where I'm going.

Our other option is bouncing forward, I suppose. We can face our challenges, learn from them, grow from them, and become better versions of ourselves.

My mentor, speaker Darren LaCroix, put it best in his award-winning speech: "As we are headed towards our goals we will reach a point where our feet will get stuck. We are so afraid of the ouch, we forget that when we lean forward and take a risk.... and fall on our face. We still... make... progress. Go ahead, fall on your face.... Fall forward!"

Let's use an example that everyone should be familiar with: *A Christmas Carol*. Just a heads up though: I'm going to be referring to the Muppet version, because that's how I roll. The story is the same, so if you haven't seen the Muppet version, you can still follow along.

In the beginning, Scrooge is an awful, miserly, cranky, old bastard who takes advantage of the frog and rats that work for him. He pays them poor wages, keeps the threat of the "unemployment line" hanging over their heads, refuses to ration out extra coal for the furnace, and makes them work on Christmas. He refuses to give to the poor, has no relationship with his family, and mocks a homeless bunny for his lot in life. No bueno.

Then, the ghosts show up. Christmas Past, Christmas Present, and Christmas Future (who is creepy as all hell), stop by to help Scrooge reflect on how he lives his life, and what will happen if he goes unchanged. He wakes up the next morning, gets ready for work and goes right back to torturing his employees and ignoring the poor.

Wait. What? No he doesn't. Because that would make a shitty story!

Here is what actually happens: Scrooge wakes up, grateful to be alive and to have the opportunity to right the wrongs he has committed. He donates to the poor, shows kindness and compassion to that adorable bunny, and brings a turkey the size of Fozzie Bear to the Crachets' house so that the frog and the pig can feed their wonderful, genetically impossible, frog-and-pig children.

Scrooge faces his challenge and bounces forward. He is a changed man. When you face your conflict, when life kicks you in the ass, will you embrace it and become better for it, or will you stick your head in the sand and become one of those "What the hell happened to them" people?

What makes the difference?

Are certain people born with an ability to handle stress better than others? I'm not a doctor (but I did stay at a *Holiday Inn Express* last night - sorry, had to. Do you remember those commercials?). Anyway, I'm not a doctor, but there is quite a bit of research out there showing that some people are hardwired to withstand stress better than others.

Here's some research on that:

> Science has shown that those individuals considered most "resilient" have a healthier stress response. A study called <u>Dynamic Neural Activity During Stress Signals Resilient Coping</u> by Rajita Sinha, Cheryl M. Lacadie, R. Todd Constable, and Dongju Seo studied 30 healthy people by putting them in an fMRI scan session and showing them either stressful images (like people being physically hurt) or neutral images (like household items). "When you get stressed, it's not brief - it goes on for a little bit," Sinha says. "And that's the state in which the brain has to figure out what to do."

Researchers then asked the participants about how they coped with stress (eating, alcohol, arguments). While participants were exposed to the stressful images, researchers saw an increase in activity in the ventral medial prefrontal cortex (that's the area that handles emotional regulation).

> "People who had more neuroflexibility and neuroplasticity in this region were also less likely to be binge drinkers and emotional eaters, and they were less likely to respond to stress in an emotionally destructive way," Sinha says. "The greater the magnitude of the change in the neural signal, the more active copers they were," she says. "The results suggest that this part of the prefrontal cortex is involved in wresting back control during times of stress — a key aspect to resilience." <u>Stress Resilience Brain Anxiety.</u>

What about the rest of us? Are we screwed? Should we throw in the towel and request a nice jacquard fabric for our padded walls? I don't think that will be necessary. It's been my experience that you can learn to be resilient. That there are certain qualities that you can develop, tools that you can gather, and characteristics that you can foster in order to rock out at this party we call "life."

Just to backtrack a moment. Lest you believe that I am one of those blessed people hardwired for inner peace and tranquility - I'm not. At four years old, my parents put me in therapy to deal with their impending divorce. The therapist's exact words: "I've never seen a stressed out 4-year-old." So trust me, what I'm sharing with you is from years of experience, not amazing genes.

I like to think about this book as "Coconut Oil for the Soul." Hang in there for a moment, I promise I'm going somewhere with this. Think about the dead of winter. You forget to refill your humidifier, the heat is blasting at full force, you run out of body butter and your skin starts taking on the consistency of rice paper. Not only can you scratch the word "dry" in your arm, but you begin looking at every object in your life as a dangerous weapon that can scratch you, cut you, and make you bleed. Your sweet little Fido is now sporting Freddy Kruger-esque claws, and you're not sure how, but a strong wind just caused your arm to spout blood like a gluttonous mosquito. My friend, your skin is no longer resilient. It's weakened to the point where it can no longer withstand minor injuries. Refer back to the first definition of resilience.

You know how to handle this. You whip out your smartphone, call up your *Amazon* app, and order a vat of moisturizer. In two hours, a barrel of shea butter lands on your doorstep and you don your favorite birthday suit and dive in. Ahhhh... relief.

Let's get back to your emotional well-being, shall we? When we are "moisturized," we can deal with the butthead that cuts us off in traffic, we can handle the pharmacy being out of our favorite shampoo; and we can laugh at the dog that shows his love by leaving a half-eaten dead bird in the middle of the kitchen.

When we are emotionally raw, we end up on our knees in a buffet screaming, "Why me?" because they just served someone else the last piece of cherry pie. (What? Where did you hear that story? That never happened to me after a breakup...)

You need coconut oil for the soul! And it's coming, I promise. You don't even have to wait two hours for it to be delivered.

Surviving to Thriving

Chapter 1

How Do I Use This Book?

Well, reader - I'm glad you asked!

When I was outlining this book, I tried to put it in some semblance of order. But the truth is, this isn't a sequential process. You don't need to read the chapters in the order they are presented. If you feel like hopping around like a drunken frog, I support that. In fact, you don't even have to master all eleven strategies. Here's why:

- They may not all pertain to your specific situation (but that doesn't mean they might not in the future).

- Some of them may make you feel icky inside. If it doesn't feel right, go with your gut.

- You might still be working on mastering some of the strategies, but really excel at some others.

My suggestion is to find seven that you really like and believe that you can rock, and pour your now well-lubricated heart and soul into them. Why seven? Because I like that number. Yeah, that's the only reason. If you want to go with six or eight, do it.

I do have to ask something: Read the Chapter 2 on the five stages of grief before you go on to the others. I think it's important to fully understand what happens when you face a universal boot to the butt. It will also help you comprehend the process, and fully experience the process, so you don't find yourself, years from now, wondering why you are still stuck on something.

Exercises

At the end of every chapter, I have included an exercise to reinforce the lesson and put it into action. You may be resistant to doing this. I know I usually am. I have read self-help book after self-help book and you know what happens if you don't do any work during it? You get nothing out of it. I like to tell myself, "I will read it through once and then go back and read it again while doing all the exercises." But then I get another book, and I never go back for that second round. So please, do the exercises... the first time around.

There is one other bit of business to attend to. What if this book doesn't resonate with you?

I can accept that my witty banter and awkward use of metaphor may not appeal to everyone's sensibilities. Or perhaps you got turned off because I curse like a sailor. I will survive to live another day. I want what is best for you and whatever will help you overcome your challenges. If that's not my book, so be it. But I have a favor to ask:

I'm really into the environment, so if you decide that this book will not become your lifeline for the next 50-some-odd years, please reuse or recycle it. Need some suggestions for how to reuse it?

- Line the bottom of your parrot's bird cage with it. (Just don't be surprised if he starts spouting my wisdom.)

- Use it to fix a wobbly table leg or as a door stop.

- Cut a hole in the center of the pages and hide something in there.

- Give it as a gift to someone who might enjoy my smart - assery, (It's a word, don't question me).

- Use it to practice your balance while walking straight (bonus points if you play music from *My Fair Lady* in the background).

- Give it to your yellow lab to distract her from chewing on the couch.

If none of these ideas work for you, at the very least, recycle it. Our earth has taken enough of a beating without my book ending up in a landfill.

If you are reading this on your Kindle, trash it, baby!

Are you ready to learn how to lather up and weather the shitstorm of life? Read on, my friends. Read on.

Chapter 2

The Drowning Giraffe

You have my word, no giraffes were harmed in the making of this book.

So... why is this chapter titled The Drowning Giraffe?

Because the first time I was introduced to the Five Stages of Grief, it was through a cartoon created by Robot Chicken, starring Seth Green as a giraffe who has gotten himself into a bit of a sticky wicket. I highly suggest putting this book down for three minutes (no more!), and Googling "Quicksand" by Robot Chicken. You won't be sorry you did.

I will be here, whistling the theme to Jeopardy. Doo doo doo doo. Doo doo doo. Doo doo doo doo do...

Oh good! Welcome back. Did you love it? To be fair, it probably wasn't the first time that I learned about grief (I have a Bachelor's and a Master's in Psychology — I'm not completely talking out of my ass here), but it was certainly the one that stuck out.

Before I go into more detail about each of the five stages, I want to explain to you why I requested that you read this chapter first. I honestly believe that if you don't go through the grief, if you try and put on a brave face and be all "Nah, I'm cool. Ain't nothing gonna break my stride" (I'm showing my age here, aren't I?), you are doomed to wander an emotional purgatory until you accept the suckage, process your feelings (admit it, you just uttered "blech"), and come out the other side.

I speak from experience, Grasshopper. Recent experience actually. A little over a year ago, I was laid off from my job. Now this wasn't just any job. This was THE JOB. This was the job that utilized and challenged every aspect of my very being. This was the job that had me eager to hop out of bed in the morning and reflecting on the difference I made in the world when I went to sleep at night. This was the job that I not only rocked, I rocked it so hard that little music notes would rain down from the sky. Okay, maybe not that last one, but it was truthfully the job that I would do even if I wasn't being paid. I know this, because I'm still doing it... even though I don't get paid.

When my boss told me that the company couldn't afford my salary anymore, we had a good cry, a good hug, and I went on my merry way. I cried a bit in the car (I'm a master at driving while crying), left a voicemail for my mentor, called my parents to assure them that everything would be okay, picked up some raffle prizes for an upcoming event, and went home. By the time I got home, my coach returned my call and we ticked off the positive aspects of the experience:

- the universe was telling me now was the time to start my business;

- as an entrepreneur I would never be laid off again;

- I could get unemployment while I built the foundation of my company;

- I had the opportunity to work in the most amazing job;

- I could still do the work I was doing, just on a smaller scale.

The next morning, I woke up, applied for unemployment, started searching for a mentor for my new business, and got to work.

Raise your hand if you know what I didn't do. (Now put your hand down, especially if you are in public).

That's right, I didn't grieve. I didn't follow the stages that our long-necked friend laid out for us. Instead, I squashed down all of my feelings, waived off emotion, and trudged on. And because of that, I'm going to say that I lost about six months of useful working time. My head just wasn't in the right place — I was wandering through emotional purgatory, refusing to accept the suckage that had befallen me. If you are someone who believes that we are responsible for attracting everything in our lives, then I suppose you could say I attracted a potentially fatal car accident into my life as well (spoiler alert, I didn't die).

It wasn't until I was laid up for a few weeks, with a concussion and staples in my head, that I was forced to reflect on the loss. And that's exactly what it was. Not the loss of a job. Of course that was part of it, but this was more. When I had been laid off in the past, it was 70% "Oh crap how do I pay my bills now" and 30% "Good riddance! I never liked you bastards anyway." This job, on the other hand was about 40% "How will I pay my bills" and about 60% "But this is my identity" (we will talk a little bit more about identity in chapter 11).

It took a few weeks of being literally unable to focus on any tasks in order to see the one thing that had been right in front of my face for months: This sucks. Straight up, no arguing the fact, I lost something I loved. I lost who I thought I was, and that out right SUCKED. I didn't go through the five stages when it first happened (although I had been denying that it was coming for months), which meant I had to go through them months later.

What's the takeaway here? You have to go through the five stages of grief before moving forward. If you try to stuff your feelings down, if you try to pretend like it's okay, you can handle it, you're tough... you're still going to deal with those five stages at some point. They are as inevitable as death, taxes, and losing just one sock in your dryer after each cycle.

When are you likely to experience the five stages of grief?

I would venture to guess that with any change, there will be some aspect of grieving. Even if the change is ultimately good (and you can see that through the haze), we are creatures of habit and any kind of change gets our panties in a bunch. We view change as loss. Loss of what we had, who we were, who we had, etc. So it's not just the obvious scenarios, losing your job, having a loved one pass away, having an illness or life-altering accident, that cause these feelings, it can really be anything. (Cheery, isn't it).

But like those public service announcements in the 80's: The More You Know... (Was there an ending to that commercial? ...The better? ... The more money you will earn?...The less likely you are to be eaten by wildebeests?). I digress. The more you know about what you are about to face (and need to face), the better.

One of my absolute favorite quotes is from Winston Churchill: "If you are going through hell, keep going."

Simple. Brilliant. Don't stop.

Let's dive into these five stages of grief and learn what there is to learn.

These were first identified or proposed by Elisabeth Kübler-Ross in her 1969 book, <u>On Death and Dying</u>. Mourning is not isolated to a specific culture, religion, personality type, etc. It is a universal human emotion. (If you've ever watched a family pet run around the house looking for a loved one that has passed, or seen them rest their head on a fellow animal that has died, you will see that it's not just a human emotion).

Shit. Things just got really deep. Sorry about that. Think about a sloth wearing a sweater. That should cheer you back up.

Since I mentioned religion, why do you think every single religion has such elaborate death rituals? We've gotten past the days where coins were put on the eyes' of the dead to pay for passage on the River Styx. Now, we have wakes, sit Shiva, follow the rules of Antyesti (Hindu), etc., to help the families of the deceased process their grief. It's not for the dead. The guy that passed away... yeah, he doesn't care. It's the people who love him that need to find solace and closure.

These stages of grief are different for everyone, so please don't judge if someone processes grief differently than you. The timeline is different for each person, the order in which they experience the stages may be different, their reaction to the loss may be different. These stages are more of a guideline and less of a road map. In later interviews, Kubler-Ross admitted that she regretted writing the stages as she did, because people saw them as a "right and wrong way" to grieve.

You will process in your own way, in your own time. My goal in explaining these steps to you is not to teach you how to grieve, but rather to give you the space (both emotional and temporal) to come to a place of acceptance, rather than being stuck in a life-long struggle with your loss. Think of them as nothing more than an alternative to stuffing down your feelings.

One more word of advisement and then I'll get to it. If your grief is so severe that you are contemplating hurting yourself or others... this book ain't gonna help. Find a therapist, find a support group, find a professional — and get help immediately. Thoughts of suicide are no joke and they should not be dealt with lightly.

Okay, I think we are ready to dive in. Things are about to get pretty deep. I apologize in advance but it must be done. I'm going to throw some humor in, partly for your protection, and partly for mine. Why don't you go grab a chocolate bar to nibble on while we traverse this landscape of suckage.

The Five Stages of Grief include:

Denial

Anger

Bargaining

Depression

Acceptance

1) Denial: If you've ever found yourself uttering the words, "No, there must be some mistake," you have experienced denial. You've been given bad news. Perhaps the test results came back and you've got cancer. Maybe your son was involved in a car accident and he couldn't be saved. Maybe the company you've worked for for the last twenty years is closing their doors. No matter what the news, you (at first), can't accept it. Your brain is working to process the information, and the only way it can do that is to come up with alternatives. Maybe the doctor is looking at the wrong file and your biopsy really came back negative. Maybe that wasn't your kid in the car and he's about to come walking through the door, baseball cap

askew, confused at why everyone seems so somber. Maybe your boss is just playing a super-cruel April Fool's joke on you. That guy's always been quite the prankster.

This is our brain's first defense mechanism. It's perfectly normal, and for a period of time, even healthy. However, as with any defense mechanism, it should only be temporary and it shouldn't prevent you from taking action. I'll give you an unhealthy example of this as a coping mechanism.

I mentioned before that I was laid off from the job to end all jobs. The pièce de résistance. It was a huge blow to my world, but it wasn't unexpected. My boss and I had had conversations for months about the financial state of the company, and how the owners were taking money out of their personal savings to make payroll each week. The healthy reaction would've been to deal with my grief at that moment, mourn the impending loss, and then start putting out feelers for another job that I could love.

Instead, I chose to ignore it. I denied the possibility of being laid off. Something would come through. We'd get a big client, another investor would step up and help us through these rocky times, the freaking financial fairy would visit and sprinkle us with magic money dust. Things were going to be okay. I denied the thought that I could be without a job, ignored the potential for financial and emotional ruin that was poking its head out from behind a wall, Cheshire smile spread across its face, screaming, "Here's Johnny!" It wasn't until the conversation started with, "It's over" and ended with, "Is two weeks fair?" that I finally began to accept that the financial fairy was vacationing in the South of France and no miracles were in store.

In retrospect, it's probably a good thing that I denied reality as long as I did. If I had started looking for another "job," I wouldn't be writing this book. I wouldn't be embarking on a new career, and I don't think that I would be following my heart and changing the world for the better. That being said, I still don't recommend ignoring or denying bad news. If nothing else, it causes a lot of unnecessary stress. You are strong. You can and will face what the world is giving you.

2) Anger: If you find the F-bomb dropping raining down from your mouth more than a rap artist in a traffic jam, you may be experiencing anger. This too is natural. You've stopped denying the reality of the situation and now you are just pissed. The anger could be directed at anyone, from the person who left you (be it of their own volition or not), to the poor, unsuspecting mailman that is about to spend his afternoon dislodging a pack of coupons from his ass. Maybe you are pissed at your boss for mismanaging the company for so many years and putting your well-being in jeopardy. This is normal, and just another stage or emotional state that you need to go through.

If a loved one has passed, you may feel resentful that they left (if only they had taken better care of themselves; if only they took up knitting instead of base jumping), and then have the added guilt about feeling resentful. It's normal. However it's also a cycle. You may also become more angry because of your guilt.

I've always loved this quote from the Buddha:

"Holding on to anger is like grasping a hot coal with the intention of throwing it at someone else; you are the one who gets burned."

Normal, useful, and protective. Yet, just like denial and Goldenseal Root, it's only healthy when used in small doses.

3) Bargaining: We've all done it. When you've laid on your bed speaking to your higher power and said: "God (Universe, angels, Vishnu, etc.) if you just bring back my

child, take back that diagnosis, keep my job safe, I will make a change." Maybe you offer to attend religious services more, be a more loving parent, take the dog for daily walks, stop scrolling through Facebook at your desk, etc. No matter what deal you try to make, what's done is done. This is just your brain's way of trying to regain control over a situation that you feel helpless, frightened, and vulnerable about.

4) Depression: Sometimes referred to as, "anger turned inwards." Our brains are beginning to wrap themselves around the loss... but that doesn't mean we like it. We may deal with different types of depression. One pertaining to the practical or logistical changes we are enduring, such as having to pay for funeral costs, figuring out how to budget while in treatment, or looking for another job before the next mortgage payment comes due. The other type of depression is more emotionally or inwardly focused. This is how we process the actual loss; how we deal with the removal of a person from our world, or a change in identity (either health or career related).

I mentioned before that you should seek help if you are contemplating self harm. But if you are unable to perform daily functions for yourself or others, that's a good time to seek help, as well. There is nothing shameful about seeing a counselor, and nothing wrong with utilizing prescribed pharmaceuticals for short periods of time. Sometimes you just need a little help. If you are comfortable, ask family or friends for recommendations. If you'd rather not involve them, call you primary care physician for a referral.

Even if the depression is severe but not debilitating, it's still not a bad idea to have a mental health professional in your corner (preferably someone with experience in grief counseling).

5) Acceptance: You've made it. And when I say that, I don't mean that you're life is now filled with candy and

pixie dust. Acceptance doesn't mean happiness. It just means that you've made peace with the situation. This doesn't happen for everyone. Some people may continue through life angry, depressed, even denying their situations.

I had a conversation with a loved one once (I won't go into details so as not to hurt them). I asked her, "When are you going to let your abuser stop hurting you?" (The abuser was deceased for eight years at the time of this talk). Her answer: "When I'm dead."

Mic drop.

Acceptance might just be a choice. I believe that there comes a time (or a fork in the road) where you need to make the decision to accept the past and carve a new future for yourself, or to carry a chip the size of a Buick around on your shoulder and blame all future experiences and disappointments on Chip. The question is, what choice will you make?

Phew! We made it through.

That was some deep shit right there. Struggle: supposedly that's what makes the good parts of life as good as they are. You need the bad in order to appreciate the good.

That doesn't mean that it doesn't suck while we are going through it. The good news is we get through it. The rest of this book is about some practical ways to do just that: get through it. Hop on your surfboard of life and let's ride the waves.

Exercise

It's time to do some soul searching (don't whine, this will be good for you). In order to find out where you are going, we need to take stock of where you are. Review the steps above and then insert your specific scenario into it.

The challenge I'm facing right now is:

_____

The way I have experienced stage 1 (Denial) is:

_____

The way I have experienced stage 2 (Anger) is:

_____

The way I have experienced stage 3 (Bargaining) is:

_____

The way I have experienced stage 4 (Depression) is:

_____

The way I have experienced stage 5 (Acceptance) is:

_____

Surviving to Thriving

Chapter 3

Charlotte's Web of Emotional Support

You know that friend that comes to town once a year, involves you in a whirlwind of debauchery and then flits out of town, leaving a wake of hangovers and bad decisions? Yeah, that's not who this chapter is about. There are those people in your life who you call to have a good time: to celebrate a victory, peruse the town for tail, and party like it's 1999. Then there are the people that you call at 4 am to pick you up off the bathroom floor when the reality of your divorce has hit; who will hold your hand while you have staples removed from your head; and who drive you to your chemotherapy appointments. These are the people that make up your web of emotional support.

Don't get me wrong, it's great to have both types of people in your life. You just need to know who is who when crisis strikes.

In their book, <u>Resilience: The Science of Mastering Life's Greatest Challenges</u>, Charney and Southwick discuss the importance of having a strong network of social support. "Very few highly resilient individuals are strong in and by themselves," Southwick says. "You need support." There are even neurobiological elements to social support. Research has shown that when people are exposed to a stressor in a lab and have a friend in the room with them, their heart rate and blood pressure don't go up quite as much as if they're alone.

So who makes up your web? It may be your immediate family, less immediate family, friends, mentors, religious leaders, even a trusted boss. And here's the kicker... it may change from one situation to the next. A quick example: I have a woman in my life who has been my sounding board most of my life. I'm an only child and she is the closest thing to a sister that I have ever had. Theoretically, I should go to her with everything, right?

Wrong. I remember the day that I called her, all excited to say that I was going to be a professional speaker. Her immediate response: what makes you an expert? Now I'm sure she didn't intend for that comment to cut me down, but it did. In subsequent conversations, she always made suggestions for other ways to make money. Support system for my speaking career? I think not. Still someone I go to for almost everything else, absolutely.

Sometimes your family sucks. I said it. Not everyone was born to amazingly supportive parents. Some parents are judgmental, bitter, angry, and resentful when their children strive for things that they themselves have not accomplished. It's okay if you need to admit that your parents aren't part of your web. That's why we have friends. They are the family we get to choose.

Speaking of the family we get to choose, let's not overlook our furry little friends. A study published in the Journal of Personality and Social Psychology, found that the emotional benefits of pet ownership can be equal to those of human friendship. If you've ever cried into your dog's fur (for a while there, I think my dog was starting to mold), had a cat butt her head up against you during rough times, or pet a bunny while stressing you already know this. (Note: the study only focused on dogs and cats, but whatever furry, scaly, or finned creature helps you, I say go for it.) The best part about animals... they never give you advice. They only give you support and love.

My dream is to set up camping tents throughout town with adoptable kittens or puppies. Donate to the animal rescue and you get "fur therapy." Climb in the tent and get loved on for however long. Depression - cured. Anxiety - cured. World Peace - yep, that should do it.

Maybe you don't have family (or they suck), all of your friends are "good time" friends, and you are dangerously allergic to fur. Now what? I won't get into the religion discussion, but I will say that congregations, no matter what religion they believe in, are gatherings of people that theoretically are there to support each other. Your church, synagogue, mosque, whatever, may provide solace during rough times.

Quick note about a higher power: Whether you believe in God, Buddha, Mohammad, the Flying Spaghetti Monster, or Joe Pesci - find something to believe in.

That's it. Religious talk over. If I offended you, refer back to the How to Use this Book section in the Introduction.

Finally, if you are looking for that empathy, for the "I've been there" or "I'm there right now" type of support, consider a support group. There are support groups organized around almost every disease, crisis, situation, stage of life, etc. You name it, they've got a support group for that. Trying to quit alcohol or drugs, check. Struggling with your sexual identity, check. Lost a loved one, check. Diagnosed with cancer, check. You can find in-person support groups, virtual groups, groups by phone, whatever format you are comfortable with.

One of the biggest ironies of depression is that, at a time when you need support most, you feel (and make yourself) the most isolated. If you are dealing with depression or grief, you may feel as if you are the only person alive that has ever experienced such intense pain. You may feel as if your friends and family won't understand, or you don't want to burden them, or even worse, they don't care. You probably feel alone.

You are not alone. (Are you singing Michael Jackson now?)

Pop quiz: What's the difference between sympathy and empathy?

Go ahead, I'll just hum the Jeopardy theme again.

Sympathy is feeling bad for someone. Feeling sorrow or pity for their situation. Empathy, is putting yourself in someone else's shoes (or knowing how they feel, because you have been there). Some of the people that you go to for help may only be capable of sympathy. They may not understand what it's like to go through divorce, lose a child, be diagnosed with an illness — but that doesn't mean that they don't care.

A quick story about the power of empathy in certain situations. A few years ago, a friend of mine called in a near panic. She was eight months pregnant at the time. I had never given birth to a child (and probably never will). Here's how the conversation went down:

Friend: Sheryl, I'm really scared. I'm afraid that it's going to hurt.

Me: Ummm, hun... I'm not really sure why you called me.

Friend: I'm just really scared right now.

Me: Don't you have a friend or someone that has been through this? Maybe someone with two kids that knew what it took and chose to do it again?

Friend: I'm just really scared.

Me: You should be. A human being is about to come ripping out of your vagina.

Friend: I don't know why I called you.

Everyone needs support.

It doesn't matter where you go to get it. The people who are able to weather the storms of life are the ones who are surrounded by loving family, friends, and furry creatures. Take stock of the relationships that you have, and nurture them whenever possible.

How do you do that?

Ask any 1950's sitcom mom. The best way to have a friend is to be a friend. That doesn't mean that you should be at someone's beck and call at all hours of the night, but when the people in your life are in need of support, offer it. When they need a ride home from the doctor, drive them. And when they need to be lifted off the bathroom floor at four in the morning and held until sunrise, push up your sleeves and prepare to spend the next day tired.

Some other ways to make and keep friends? Don't be a dick. I hope that this isn't a challenging concept. Basically, don't lie to your friends, don't cheat with their partners, don't talk about them behind their backs, and don't insult them to their faces, either. Pretty common sense stuff, right? So I will just leave it as: Don't be a dick.

Exercise

It's time to actually take stock of your support system. I want you to list at least ten people that you can go to in times of trouble. Of course, this is easier to do when you aren't feeling depressed, but it's still worthwhile if you are.

Remember: this can be family, friends, your golden retriever, the people at your house of worship, a therapist, a coach, etc.

And if there are people in your life that are good for some topics, but not for others, write that down, too. Whatever you do, don't call me about childbirth.

Chapter 4

Warning Signs, Wake-Up Calls, and Wombats

There is nothing more satisfying, more gratifying, and more useless than pointing fingers. When something goes wrong in our lives we LOVE to place blame. We love to say, "Well if he hadn't (fill in the blank)" or "It's her fault I (fill in the blank)" to justify our lot in life. Maybe your wife cheated on you, maybe your boyfriend abuses you, maybe your boss takes advantage of your work ethic and is running you into the ground. Whatever is going on in your life... I bet it is someone else's fault.

Let me tell you why that's bullshit.

A quick dive into my history here. I was married what seems like a lifetime ago, and it ended in an explosion that puts the Death Star to shame. He was a hot mess from day one. Swimming in debt, criminal record that had been sealed (but apparently not well), and mommy issues up the wazoo. It was as if the stars had aligned to bring me the perfect "project" (I hope my sarcasm is dripping heavily enough from the page — it's always a challenge with the written word).

Stay with me here, I don't want you skimming over this to get to the epic blast at the end.

He never hid any of his issues from me (at least not at that point). So I went into this marriage fully aware of how much money he owed the world (and actually paid it off for him so we could start fresh), aware of his propensity shall we say, for skirting the law (are you getting curious yet?), and aware that he was constantly one step away from rebelling against an overbearing family. Let's go ahead and call this the "warning sign" portion of our title. There were plenty of signs, red flags, giant elephants in the room wearing unitards with bright red sequins spelling out, "Run like hell before it's too late," but I chose to ignore those.

I also chose to ignore wake-up calls during our marriage. Like when he bought me a $2000 piece of jewelry for our anniversary (yeah, you're all oohs and ahhs until I tell you that he couldn't afford it and I ended up paying off my own stupidly priced jewelry). I slept right through that wake up call. Or what about the time I found out he'd opened a credit card that I didn't know about — didn't hear the buzzer. I even hit the snooze button if you will, when I found out that he opened the credit card to charge his online gambling habit. And I just straight up threw the alarm clock across the room when I found out he was doing online gambling to cover up for a rather expensive online porn addiction.

Ignorance is bliss? Nope.

Ignorance is fricking stupid.

If I had paid attention to the warning signs, listened to the wake up calls, been awake and aware of what was happening, I could've avoided the Wreckoning (don't bother looking that up in the history books). What's that you might ask?

That's the day that my phone rang and all my husband could utter was, "I'm in big trouble."

POP QUIZ:

Raise your hand if you can guess what happened. (Seriously, did you fall for that again? You know I can't see you right?)

I'll give you three guesses - I'm actually going to *give* them to you since I can't hear you either.

a) Prostitution - he picked up a hooker at the local 7-11.

b) Drugs - he got caught with a kilo of cocaine in his trunk (does cocaine come in kilos? Can you tell I don't know anything about drugs?)

c) Shoplifting - he got tired of spending my money to buy me gifts and instead just stole them.

Wrong!

None of that would have made for as good a story. Nope. My honey, baby bear, shnookey wookums was arrested for soliciting a minor online.

Apparently our wedding officiant should've stated the conditions "Until death... or pedophilia do us part."

Now there are two ways that we can look at this story (three if you include abject horror). We can go with the "How could he do this to me" camp, or the "How could I do this to me?"

Wait, what?

Let's back up a second.

Remember, I read a few self-help books when I was going through my divorce...

Actually I read EVERY self help book while I was going through my divorce. My bedstand looked like the library at Hay House.

But one piece of advice really stood out for me. It cautioned against ever labeling yourself as a victim. When you say that things "happen to you," you give away your power. If you believe that your partner, your parents, your best friend, your kids, the neighbor's cross-eyed poodle, etc. are at fault for everything that happens in your life, you give away your power to ever change your circumstances. After all, you will always be at the whim of that visually challenged poodle.

There is a big difference between accepting responsibility and accepting fault. I wasn't at fault for my husband's crimes. I didn't suggest he try to sleep with a thirteen year old. I didn't drive him to her house, and as a lawyer said to me when I asked if I could be held legally culpable, I didn't dress up like a child when we had sex. It was not my fault that he did what he did. I could even whine and say that he did it to me, threw my world into a tizzy and ruined my life. Of course, that would suggest that the next person who came along could do the same thing.

Or, I could take responsibility for being in the relationship that I was in, despite knowing everything I did. I could take responsibility for getting married to a man that I had no business marrying, and allowing him to put me in a dangerous and (teetering on the edge) situation. That option would suggest that I wasn't going to let it happen again.

I stood at the airport four years later, waiting for my brand new, long-distance boyfriend to skulk off the plane after having almost missed it due to a night of partying that I had nicely suggested he cut out of early to make his flight. He got off the plane and we kissed... and then I punched him in the stomach.

"Just so you know," I said, "if you hadn't gotten on that plane, we were done."

"You aren't going to take any shit, are you?"

"Nope. I've taken enough shit in my life."

Have you taken enough shit in yours?

You might not like this, but I'm going to say it anyway.

Stop calling yourself a victim. You are where you are today because of the decisions you made yesterday, last week, and 16 years ago. Be it that you are miserable at work, divorced, overweight, etc. If you continue to believe that others dictate who you are and how you live, then things will never change. The day that you accept responsibility for your existence is the day that you can lift your sword to the sky and scream "I have the power!" (If you have no idea what I'm talking about right now, head on over to Google and look up He-Man. I can wait).

Got your sword? Now what?

Well, for starters - just like history (which is doomed to repeat itself), maybe you should learn from your mistakes and make some better decisions. (You didn't hate me before, but you are starting to, right?) I love Einstein's definition of insanity: doing the same thing over and over, and expecting a different result.

What have you tried before? And how did that go for you?

Now, this wasn't about beating yourself up. Put down the whip, there will be no self-flagellation today. It doesn't help to place blame on yourself either. This is about identifying the warning signs that you ignored, and not ignoring them in the future. This is about admitting that you have control over your own life, and using that control to make things better. This is about approaching every situation with the knowledge that you can affect the outcome.

Rom Brafman talks about Tunnelers in his book <u>Succeeding When you are Supposed to Fail</u>. Now, this isn't a sci-fi term out of *Dune*. Tunnelers are basically people who find a way to tunnel through all the shit in life and come out the other side smelling like roses. They are able to do this, in part, because of this Limelight Effect. Not a supercool club in Manhattan (I have no idea if this still exists, but it was a cool gothic church converted into a night club and music venue), the Limelight Effect refers to where you place the spotlight in your own life.

"In life, we have a psychological limelight that focuses our attention," says Brafman. "Is our limelight pointed at ourselves or is it directed at the world around us? In other words, do we view ourselves as the protagonist in our lives or do we pay more attention to people and events around us?"

There are people with external limelights who give credit to others for all the good that happens in their life and blame others for all the bad. As you can imagine, they don't do so well with challenges. Then, there are the Tunnelers with their internal limelights. They take responsibility for what has happened in their lives and they take steps to correct or improve it.

Afraid you might be an external limelighter? Don't worry, there are ways that you can shift the limelight or the "locus of control," as psychologist Julian Rotter who discovered the phenomenon, called it. "One strategy is to develop sensitivity to external-oriented perspectives," said Brafman. "Instead of focusing on how others have wronged us, we can ask ourselves, "Where am I in all of this? What responsibility can I take moving forward?" This doesn't mean that we should absolve others from responsibility. It simply means that no matter what happens, in the end the only person we have full control over is ourselves.

Ready to do some work?

Hey! Where are the wombats?

Exercise

1) Make a list of a few of the events, hardships, tragedies, etc. that you have experienced in your life and dig deep to find the warning signs that were there from day one. Also list if there were any wake-up calls (smaller incidences) that led to the big disappointment.

2) What could you have done differently to have achieved a different outcome from those experiences?

3) What can you do in the future to avoid experiencing more hardship?

Surviving to Thriving

Chapter 5

Be a Duck

"Try not to take things personally. What people say about you is a reflection of them, not you."
– Unknown

I think a big part of resiliency is not allowing certain things to get to you in the first place. The less "slights" you have been dealt, the less you have to get over. Now you probably aren't going to like that I have to make this point, but I'm going to do it anyway.

It's time for a wake-up call (don't hit the snooze, please).

It's not all about you.

Let me say that one more time for the people in the back.

It's not all about you.

If you are like me, you have battled a lifelong case of codependency. That means that you are responsible for the actions, the happiness, the mistakes, and the pain of everyone around you. Well, not really, but that's what you think. When you look back at your life, you probably had an addict in your childhood (and have frequently attracted another one in to your adulthood) or perhaps were raised by someone with a mental illness. Either way, you were a caretaker well before you should've been, and the caretaking stretched out to the point of enabling.

If you aren't familiar with this affliction, it's not extreme cockiness or the belief that the sun revolves around you. It's more of a million-ton sense of responsibility that weighs on your shoulders, making Atlas look like he had it easy. It takes empathy to a whole new level — no longer "I've been in your shoes," but rather "Why don't you hop out of your shoes so I can hop in and take care of this for you."

How does this codependency play out in your life?

Well, you are probably an excellent worker! To the point where you end up doing other people's jobs.

You are probably a loving and caring partner. To the point where you become a martyr to the relationship and eventually get resentful for the all the give you've given, and all the take they've taken.

You may be a wonderful friend. To the point where you've helped every one of your friends move, you've pet sat for them every weekend, you rebuilt your friend's house, and dear Aunt Tilda can't figure out what to buy for their wedding because you purchased everything on their registry.

And the thing is, this actually makes you happy. You feel needed, loved, accomplished, worthwhile... and resentful as all hell.

You take what people say about you as gospel, (we will talk more about this in a later chapter) and often, you morph into someone else in order to meet their expectations. (By the way, this rarely works out well - if your friends are trying to change you into who they think you should be, they aren't friends. They are not dealing with their own issues, but rather passing them off to you).

This brings us to the first rallying cry of the recovering codependent: "That's your shit."

Say it loud, say it proud, say it with me:

"That's your shit!"

I don't mean to sound harsh (well, maybe a little harsh), but sometimes people are just deflecting their own crap onto you. Some people are able to laugh it off, realizing right away that the outburst or whatever has nothing to do with them. For us special codependent types, we instantly believe that we have wronged our fellow man and must correct it.

Sometimes though, that's just them. I remember a few years ago having a long talk with a friend (the last long talk we would have for several years). In it, he explained that I had bad energy and being around me was dragging him down.

Ummm... I'm no Happy Meal with feet, but for the most part, I'm a pretty positive, upbeat, forward-thinking individual.

I got off the phone with him shocked, appalled, hurt, and believing every word he said. I must be a negative person. I must have this storm cloud of negativity following me like the poofs of dirt that came off Charlie Brown's friend. And if I wasn't a Negative Nellie before the conversation, I sure as hell was after. I took what he said to heart and allowed it to affect who I was.

It wasn't until a week or two later when I was relaying the experience to another friend, that I realized just how wrong he was.

"Apparently, I'm really negative and it's bringing him down."

She stared, jaw dragging on the floor. "Sheryl, even in the midst of your depression, you've managed to find humor, be there for your friends, and find the good in things. That guy is out of his mind."

Oh yeah. I was pretty positive. I did find humor in almost every situation. So what happened? Was my friend "out of his mind"?

Nope. That was just his shit. In fact, that was so much his shit that a few years later when we ran into each other at a party, he actually apologized.

"I'm sorry about what I said the last time we talked. It took me a while, but I realized that those were actually my issues coming through."

Well look at that. His shit.

Can you think of any times where someone reacted to you, said something to you, or blamed something on you that perhaps had more to do with their history than your own behavior?

Of course we all have these moments in our lives when we think that someone is out to offend us personally, screw up our day, etc. In fact, I'm sure on your way to work or to pick up your kids from school, you probably crossed paths with one of these people. They might've cut you off in traffic or refused to let you in to the pickup line at your son's elementary school, and you may have reacted something like this:

"Holy (insert your preferred expletive here)! Can't you see that I'm trying to get in? Why the hell would you do that to me?"

It's that "to me" that indicates you might be taking things a bit personally. If your comment was more like, "You dumbass, go the F home," chances are that you haven't internalized it. (Good job!)

There's a more extreme version of this, well beyond what we experience in traffic or at work. It's called Paranoid Schizophrenia.

Hold on just one minute... did I just compare you to a severely mentally ill person?

No... and yes.

Here's the thing, the first lesson you learn in psychology classes is that mental illness is really a spectrum. Everyone is dealing with a little bit of it. The real problem is when it gets so severe that it interferes with your daily life. I will give you an example.

Raise your hand if you had to circle back around the block to make sure that your garage door was closed this morning (and yesterday morning, and maybe the morning before that)?

That's called Obsessive Compulsive Disorder. Don't be offended. We all engage in these behaviors from time to time. Now I don't generally worry about the garage door, (though my father will constantly turn to my stepmom halfway down the street to ask if it's closed); however, little known fact: I always do five swipes of deodorant under each arm. Not four, not six, but five. Every day. Is this interfering with my daily life? No, though I may run out of deodorant faster than others. When does it become a problem? How about if you have to do a 777-point check list before leaving the house every morning? Windows locked, doors closed, dog bed fluffed, cats have water, bed is made, television remotes are put away, toaster is unplugged, toilet seat is down, etc. But you don't do this once. You do this 7 times before you can leave the house. Guess who isn't making it to work... ever? Your mental illness is now severe enough or far enough down the spectrum that it is interfering with your daily life.

Make sense? Can I move onto Paranoid Schizophrenia now?

People that suffer from Paranoid Schizophrenia believe that the world is out to get them. They sometimes derive messages from meaningless interactions. For example, the Son of Sam, David Berkowitz, killed six people in the 1970's because he thought his neighbor's dog was instructing him to do it. Sorry, David. "Woof, woof, woof" means "Please get me a rawhide chew," not "I need you to shoot innocent people."

Ever not receive a text back from someone for a few hours? Did you spend those hours ruminating on the last text you sent, re-reading it over and over again to see if "Hey I miss you" could be misinterpreted? "Oh no! Did I move too fast? Am I suffocating them? Do they hate me now? Are they cheating on me? Are they cheating on me right now? I'm going to die alone." When you finally did hear back did you get something like, "I miss you, too. Shitty day. I dropped my phone in the toilet and missed my meeting because I had to go to the Apple store."

Yeah. Stop deriving so much meaning from everything that happens. Sometimes a lack of texting is just a technical error, and sometimes a Chihuahua is just begging for squeaky toy.

One of my young-adult clients at the mental health facility (we will call him Bob) was diagnosed with Intermittent Explosive Disorder, categorized by angry verbal outbursts, sudden aggression, and violent behavior. He would boil over and spew hot lava if someone knocked into him in the hallway, viewing it as a personal affront and an attack on his very being. I remember the day that I told him to be a duck. He looked at me with utter confusion while I explained that he needed to let the little things roll off his back. It took awhile, but we eventually turned it into a game. Bob would poke his head into my office and with flushed cheeks say "So and so laughed today when I asked a question. Can I kick his ass?" I would calmly shake my head and say "So and so hears voices... apparently very funny ones. He's not laughing at you. Be a duck." Bob would nod, his face returning to normal and before he left the office, I would call out "Hey, Bob! It's not all about you!"

And it's a constant battle. This is something that I have to remind myself at least three times a day thanks to that delightful codependency. When people are in a bad mood, it's usually not about me. When a friend goes into a tirade about something, it's not about me. When a family member loses her mind over a helpful hint regarding pregnancy and cleaning cat poop… it's not about me.

Let's say it together: "It's not about me."

Ready to put this into action?

Exercise

Write about a time when you took something extremely personally, got all bent out of shape, and then realized that it had absolutely nothing to do with you.

What challenges are you facing right now that may not have anything to do with you?

Chapter 6

At Least I'm Not On Fire!

Have you ever experienced one of those pity parties so grand it should be a pity gala? A pity fiesta? A pity hootenanny? There are guests, fruit punch (most likely spiked), a piñata, pin the tail on the whiner... Yeah, me too.

A few things in your life start to go awry and suddenly everything sucks. Your boyfriend might be cheating on you, your boss is going to fire you, even your precious pug is giving you the stink eye. It's a downward spiral of suckage and you can't escape.

Okay, you know that none of that is actually happening, right? The world hasn't conspired to give you a shitty week, you're just perceiving it that way. And for goodness sakes, your dog loves you. Go give Sparky a treat. I can wait.

Welcome back.

When we get into these, "nobody loves me, everyone hates me - I'm gonna go eat worms" moods, the world is a dark, cruel, unforgiving place and we are just stuck in it. Trust me, I've been stuck many a time. I had a friend in college who used to listen patiently to my woes and then say, "At least you aren't on fire." It actually happened just a few weeks ago, the night before I sat down to write this book.

I called up my friend Kathi for a whinefest (not to be confused with a winefest), and it was flowing like water. Being an entrepreneur is hard, I don't feel well, my boyfriend did something stupid, I'm tired, a dog peed on me while I was volunteering, I have a speech coming up that I'm unprepared for, I haven't heard back from vendors about my upcoming event, (insert guttural whining noise here).

My friend listened patiently and then said the most useful, make-me-feel-like-an-ass-hat, statement that one can possibly make.

"Wow, it looks like you've got such a great life. Amazing family, great boyfriend, nice house, awesome dog. Who could think that you've got so many problems?"

It's like the cops got called to break up my pity party.

Hmmm. She might be on to something here. Is it possible that in my period of epic whining, I forgot about all of the wonderful things in my life? Is it possible that we get more of what we focus on? Is it possible that our lives are really freaking fabulous (minus some small periods of yuck), and we should be grateful for all of the good, and stop worrying so much about the small pockets of bad?

That's gratitude, baby! If you've ever heard someone rattle off, in a sing-songy voice: "I have an attitude of gratitude," and thought about smacking them, you're not alone. Don't worry, you don't have to be cutesy or an inspirational meme with feet to be a positive person who focuses more on the good than the bad. You just have to make a conscious decision to incorporate a gratitude practice into your life.

I want to share a little bit about my practice and then give you some examples of others.

Every morning (okay, not every morning - but mostly every morning), I do yoga. I have a spare bedroom in my house that has been dedicated to all things soul feeding (does that sound like a horror movie?). I paint in there, my bathtub is in that bathroom, and I have a statue of a dog in lotus pose, reminding me to get my yoga on. I sit down on my mat, set an intention for the practice (which usually has to do with sending healing energy towards a loved one - I'm still working on setting an intention for myself). I then spend the next 20-40 minutes trying not to fall over or step on the dog who insists on being under me. When I finally get into corpse pose (a position that is supposed to elicit both physical and mental stillness), I know myself and I know my monkey mind will be doing circus acts if I don't focus on something. So I make my gratitude list. I lay there and I go through everything that I am grateful for: my family, boyfriend, friends, my amazing dog (who at this point is stretched out along side me with a paw firmly jammed in my rib cage), my home, my health, etc. After, and only after, I have given thanks and shown my appreciation for what I already have, then I ask for something else (we are talking health and happiness for my family, not a new pair of designer shoes).

Maybe you'd rather be ripped apart by angry elephants than sit down on a yoga mat; maybe you prefer to write, or draw, or pray. Whatever your brand of meditation or connection is, go for it. Some people keep a gratitude journal, making a list of all things awesome before they go to bed at night. You may choose to keep a gratitude jar, writing good things on slips of paper and pulling them out when you need a quick pick me up. Perhaps you say Grace at dinner or have children that you want to include in your gratitude practice. Sharing your gratitude with others can be even more beneficial (feeding two birds with one scone - you realize that you've got it good and someone else gets the warm fuzzies and knows that they've made an impact on your life.)

A gratitude practice can and will look different for everyone. The important thing is that you remember, daily preferably, that your life is pretty damn good. Robert Emmons, the world's leading scientific expert on gratitude, recognizes oodles of benefits from showing gratitude. These include physical benefits, psychological benefits, and social benefits. The physical benefits include improved immune system function, lower blood pressure, better sleep, and less pain. The psychological benefits are feeling happier, alive, alert, optimistic, and able to experience pleasure. And last but not least, social benefits include being more forgiving, outgoing, compassionate, helpful, and more connected (less isolated).

Let's be honest, if this was in a pill form, it would probably have tons of side effects like sexual dysfunction, loose stool, and a propensity for howling at the moon on the third Tuesday of every month. Yet people would still be lining up for it! What you've got here is the best drug ever, and it won't make you howl (unless you want to — no judgment here).

Ready to try it for yourself? Let's get to some exercises. I suggest cultivating an everyday gratitude practice for two reasons:

1) You get in the habit, and it starts to shift your mindset.

2) On the days that you feel like the world is taking a crap on you, you can refer back to your gratitude list from another day and remind yourself that not everything sucks.

Exercise

Grab a beautiful journal with gold leafing, a steno book in that awesome shade of yellow, or the back of the toilet paper wrapping (it's okay, you can read the Ikea catalog the next time you go potty, now is the time for gratitude).

I like to start out with Maslow's Hierarchy of needs. We could go into much more detail, but it's not necessary. Our first category (the bottom of the pyramid) is physiological needs.

Look up. Is there a roof over your head? Yes? Fantastic!

Are you shivering and or suffering from heat stroke? No? Chances are that you've got heating and cooling to keep you safe.

Have you had a meal recently or are you about to? Yes? Congratulations, you have food.

Are you writing on the back of the toilet paper wrapping? Good. Chances are that means that all systems are running and you've can check off the "excretion" category.

Sex is in this category as well, but I don't necessarily agree with it being here. Yes, it is wonderful. Yes, it is necessary to our well-being and our species. However, if you don't have it for a period of time, chances are that you will survive.

What's the gist here? You've got all the necessities. Let's take a moment here to be grateful for that. I don't want to be a bummer, but there are millions of people out there who are food insecure, are living in thatched cottages (if they are lucky), have bombs exploding overhead, etc. If you are physically safe and relatively comfortable, your life rocks.

But we are humans, and we want more. That's cool, too. Let's move up to the next level of the pyramid: Safety. This is a big one for us, and often the first level that gets shaken when we lose a job.

Do you have a source of income? Yes? Safety! You can pay your bills, keep a roof over your head, feed your family, etc.

If the answer is no, if you are reading this book because you lost your job and right now you are freaking the f out, take a deep breath. Do you have family? Friends? A spouse with an income? Do you have any talents or skills whatsoever that can be turned into money? (In case you read this and decided prostitution was for you — that is not what I'm talking about.) You are going to be just fine! It may be a little rocky there for a bit, but you will not be homeless, you will not be hungry, you will have what you need. I think sometimes we need someone to tell us that. You're welcome!

The safety rung of the ladder also includes health. The only time that you shouldn't check off this box is if you are struggling with a life-threatening illness. Sometimes we need to be reminded that an ingrown toenail is not a cause for panic, hysteria, or pity parties. If you are dealing with something minor, be grateful it's not something major.

If you are dealing with something major, this is a good time to be grateful for the emotional support, the medical team, your boss who is being wonderful about you taking time off, your church group for cooking dinners, your faith, etc. There are still things to be grateful for — they just might be a little more difficult to see.

Moving up the ladder, we get to Love/Belonging. Are there people in this world that care about you? Yes? Count yourself lucky. Is there currently a furry little monster snoozing next to you? Yes? Life doesn't get much better. Do you have awesome friends that you can call on? Do you have an amazingly supportive partner? Wonderful parents? This is what life is about—connections. If you have people (or animals) to lean on, your life is awesome.

The next two categories are Esteem and Self-Actualization. It's okay if you don't have those now because we are actually going to work on them later. So there. Now you can be grateful for this book.

Just remember that when everything seems its darkest, and life sucks the big one... at least you aren't on fire.

Chapter 7

Your Life Makes Me Feel Better About Mine

I had a friend that used to say that to me on a weekly basis. Every time something didn't go as planned in my world, every time an online dating match went awry, every time my ex-husband popped out of the woodwork with more proof of his dumbassery (yup, new word. Feel free to use it) - she would shake her head, smile, and say, "Your life makes me feel better about my own."

Yep, a pretty dick move, but there's actually some merit to this. I like to call this perspective. (No, you should never say this to a friend... or an enemy for that matter. Just don't say it period, ok?)

Back to the point. So perspective is about the way you look at things, the way you see things, and the point of view that you take. The day that my world exploded, I was bitching about clients at work. They were giving me a really hard time and I had to redo a job multiple times because they couldn't get their shit together. I was whining up a storm, complaining to my coworkers, ready to launch a full-on protest with pitchforks and angry villagers. Then, I got the phone call that changed my world.

Guess what didn't seem so bad anymore.

I had gained perspective. I had seen what a "bad day" actually looks like, and let me tell you, it had nothing to do with high-maintenance customers. Have you ever been going along in your little world, thinking that the deck was stacked against you, until you met someone or saw something that completely changed the way you looked at your own life?

I've got a few more examples to illustrate my point here.

During my college years I worked in a bank across the street from a retirement community, doing sales and customer service. My days revolved around explaining to senior citizens why they couldn't have a passbook account anymore (if you are under the age of thirty, you will probably have to look that up), explaining why it's not okay to overdraw your account every two weeks, and finally, explaining how the interest rate changes on a daily basis, so their interest deposits will fluctuate.

Yeah, it was fun stuff (I seriously need a special font for sarcasm). Anyway, I was used to this constant barrage of useless conversation, but one day it hit me harder than normal. A customer walked in and started to raise his voice. He checked his statement that month and his interest payment was 23 cents less than the month before. Nope, that wasn't a typo. **It was 23 cents less**. On a normal day, I probably would've assuaged his crankiness, but this wasn't a normal day. Halfway around the world, the Thai people were looking for their lost family members after a tsunami had claimed half of the country.

Twenty-three cents.

Ahhh perspective. The man kept up his bitching while I reached into my purse, took a shiny quarter out of my wallet, slid it across the desk and said, "People died today. Please come back when you have an actual problem."

In case you are wondering, no I didn't get fired, and no I have no idea why.

We have such a tendency to get wrapped up in our own problems. I'm not saying that sometimes they aren't significant. I'm not suggesting that we can never feel bad about our current situation. And I'm certainly not suggesting that things don't occasionally suck a ton. I'm just pointing out that it could always be worse.

A few months ago I was attending a charity event to benefit Make-A-Wish. I went into the show stressed. It had been a long couple of weeks. I'd had a disagreement with a friend earlier that day. I was worried about a project that I was working on. You name it, and I was complaining about it. The show was great, but it didn't quite pull me out of my self-induced funk.

Nope, I didn't stop feeling sorry for myself until I was walking out of the showroom. You see, there was a bottleneck situation at the doors and as I got up closer, I realized why. Make-A-Wish had brought one of their kids out to enjoy the show. He was probably about ten years old, looking tiny and frail as he laid in a hospital bed, hooked up to a variety of machines. A wave of sadness and guilt came over me. I never found out what was wrong with him, but it was obvious that he has never had, and will never have, a normal life. You know, suddenly all of my "problems" that I came in with became rather insignificant. Who the hell am I to complain about life, when there are people out there who have an honest-to-god struggle every day? Even as I sit down to write this, I had an emotionally rough day. But thinking back to that kid, I get goose bumps, and I realize maybe my day wasn't the best, but it could've been so much worse.

I'm not saying this to bum you out. And again, I'm not trying to take away from what you are going through. I'm just trying to show you that someone always has it worse.

A dear friend of mine, whenever she is having a "bad day," reminds herself that at least she's not driving her kids to cancer treatment.

Perspective, folks. Perspective is part of what will get you through the hard times. I will talk more about volunteering later, but a quick note about helping the less fortunate: it reminds you that there are less fortunate. You don't need to verbalize, "Looking at your life makes me feel better about my own," but seeing how others live will likely make you feel better about your own existence.

> Arianna Huffington talks about perspective in her book <u>Thrive</u>: There's nothing like putting your own problems in perspective. When you become involved in the lives of children for whom drive-by shootings are a regular occurrence, where one out of three fathers is in jail, and where there isn't enough to eat, it's much harder to worry about how you look, whether you're wearing the right clothes, whether you're pretty enough, and how thin you are.

Humans are by nature resilient creatures, but you know what else we are? Forgetful.

We all like to think that we learn our lessons after we screw up (or even better, after someone else screws up), but how many people do you know who actually learn a lesson after the first time?

I sure don't know any. We continue making the same mistakes time after time. Eventually, when we've been hit over the head enough times with the lesson, we start making changes. What does this have to do with perspective? Well, do you think I never bitched about a customer again after the phone call that changed my world?

Hell yeah I did! As soon as the dust settled from my epic upset, I went right back to having "bad days" and forgot that what I thought was a "bad day" was NOTHING in comparison with what had happened or could happen. I lost my perspective shortly after I gained it. And we all do.

So how do we keep our perspective with these goldfish-span memories that we are sporting?

I've read Don't Sweat the Small Stuff (And It's All Small Stuff), I've tried the "will it matter in a week... in a month... in 5 years," and it honestly does help.

There are a few questions that I like to ask myself (and I have to do it every time).

1) Is this life or death? If it's not, it's probably not as serious as I think it is.

2) Is this going to have a lasting impact on my life? If it's just a temporary shit show, it's probably not as serious as I think it is.

3) Have I (or has anyone I know) ever experienced something worse? If I have, chances are it's not as serious as I think it is.

Are you noticing a pattern?

As I type, I'm constantly distracted by the large bandage on my hand. I do animal rescue and yesterday I got bitten by one of the dogs that we had just pulled from the shelter. As I drove home from the event, my hand throbbing in pain and my brain firing maniacally regarding infection, nerve damage, the embarrassment of getting bitten by a dog and crying in front of people (it hurt like hell and I don't have a high threshold for physical pain), I went through all five steps of grief from: "This can't be happening, I'm going to look down and there isn't going to be a gaping hole in my hand," all the way to, "Crap. There is a big gaping hole in my hand and I will likely need antibiotics." I cried my eyes out (I told you I'm really good at crying and driving), and then had to apply the "Will it matter in a year" rule.

1) Life or death? If I don't take care of it, maybe. But I fully intend on cleaning the wound properly and taking medication if it shows any signs of infection.

2) Lasting impact? Well, there is always the possibility of nerve damage, but I am able to move my hand, so chances are no major damage occurred.

3) Have I or someone else experienced anything worse? Yep. A few months ago, two of the women in the animal rescue community were taking a pup to the park for a meet and greet with a potential adopters. No one knows if the dog got spooked by something or what, but he attacked. Both volunteers ended up in the hospital for several days, undergoing surgery, and ultimately, therapy.

Having created perspective, I went home to soak in epsom salts, apply antibacterial essential oils, and binge watch a chick series on Netflix. I also threw in a bonus of, "what did I learn from this experience?" Well, even though dogs are adorable and lovable and I will continue to squish and love them, I need to be more careful about how I approach pups that have just been pulled from the shelter, whom we have not done a full behavioral inventory on. Painful lesson learned.

Exercise

Are you ready to try it?

The challenge I am facing is:

_____.

Is it life or death? Y or N (just circle one)

Will there be any lasting impact or is this temporary suckage? Y or N (just circle one)

Have I, or has anyone I know ever, experienced something worse? Y or N (circle and then give an example):

_____

For the extra points, I learned

_____ from the experience.

Chapter 8

What's Your Cause?

I've been looking forward to writing this chapter for weeks. Not because it's got the snappiest title, or because I've got great quotes for it, but because I truly believe that there is nothing better you can do for yourself than to do something for someone else. You may have experienced the joy of watching someone open a present that you bought them, or watching them eat a delicious home-cooked meal you prepared especially for them. Watching someone experience joy that you caused — bring on the warm fuzzies!

I need to tell you why I am so gung-ho about doing for others.

As I've alluded to multiple times in this book, I used to be married. The upheaval of my life, the divorce, and the ensuing bankruptcy left me depressed. Not "I'm going to sit home for a few days and eat ice cream" depressed. Full-on clinical "I'm having a hard time getting out of bed" depression. I was 28, living in my parent's spare bedroom, broke, unemployed, my home was in foreclosure, I was single, and I didn't know a soul in Vegas besides my parents. I never contemplated suicide, but I would have happily accepted an end if it came to me naturally.

My parents came home one day to find me curled in the fetal position on the bathroom floor, my cheek pressed against the tile floor as tears streamed down my face. I couldn't stand up. Honestly, I didn't care if I ever did. I was trapped in my own head, drowning in my own depression.

My stepmom reached down and pulled me up. She looked me in the eyes and said, "Sheryl, this isn't you."

She was right. It wasn't me. But the real me had gotten so clouded by my situation and my emotions, that I lost sight of her. I felt broken, and more importantly — unfixable.

My stepmom sat with me on the couch while I dialed a therapist and made an appointment. My dog Akasha laid her snout on my lap and waited patiently as my tears soaked her fur.

Clinical depression sucks. It's sometimes described as anger turned inwards. If you've never experienced it, it's like a dark cloud looming over your head constantly. A feeling that there is nothing you can do to make things better, nothing anyone can do. In the psychology community it's called Helplessness and Hopelessness. If you've never experienced true clinical depression, count your blessings. If you have, I'm so sorry. If you are experiencing it right now, please make sure that you are seeking professional help as well as reading this book (I know I said this before, but it's no joke and I don't want anyone to suffer).

So there I was in a sauna of my own despair. The therapist recommended anti-depressants and this opened a whole new can of worms. I'd gone through all the schooling, I'd taken the classes on the biochemistry of the brain. I knew that there were physiological changes to the brain that occurred during depression. I also knew that anti-depressants could counteract those changes... that didn't matter. I can honestly say that I thought taking pills to change your mood was the weak way out. Not being able to get off the bathroom floor gives you a different perspective. I reluctantly took the pills, knowing that they were going to take almost a month to kick in.

Here's where things get good. Needing to keep myself busy, needing to get out of my own head, I decided to take my loyal pup out for a day of fun in the sun (plus she needed to dry out. I was crying into her fur a lot and she smelled quite musty). We found a pet festival nearby and hopped in the car. The sights, the smells, the grass! My dog enjoyed it, too. There were vendors, food, other dogs to sniff (she did that, not me), and a bunch of animal rescues. I started talking to one called Foreclosed Upon Pets. This was back in 2008 during the housing crisis and I wasn't the only one who had to walk away from their house. The difference though, was that when I left, I took my dog with me. The volunteers at the table explained that real estate agents, bank reps, neighbors, were going into foreclosed houses and finding family pets left behind to die.

Messed up.

This organization started to rescue, rehabilitate, and re-home those pets. I didn't know how, but I knew that I wanted to help. Akasha was my solace throughout the whole misadventure. The thought of leaving her behind... well there just wasn't even a possibility. I asked the volunteers what they needed and they responded in unison: MONEY!

Yeah well, I certainly didn't have any of that. But I figured I could probably get some. I went home with a skip in my step that hadn't been there in months. I didn't know how to help myself, but I could still help someone else (several someones... several furry someones actually). I began organizing a yard sale with the full support of the animal rescue. Volunteers came out of the woodwork to help me gather donations, spread the word, and the day of the event there were about twenty people standing outside my parents' house at 5 am, ready to help sell.

We made over a thousand dollars in just a few short hours. The animal rescue was ecstatic, and my life was forever changed. I had new friends, I had new skills, and for the first time in a long time, I was happy. From there I started volunteering at adoption events, running tables at community events, and eventually planning my own fundraiser (and raising over $5k) for Hearts Alive Village.

By the time the meds kicked in, I was already in a much better place. I had found a way to get out of my own head, to stop focusing on my problems, and to contribute to something larger than myself. With every furry little life that I saved, they saved me right back.

But you don't have to believe me (though I hope that if you've made it this far in the book, you do believe me). There are scores of research and scientific studies that tout the benefits of volunteering. It's like this well-kept secret that shouldn't be well kept.

In The Hidden Gifts of Helping, Stephen G. Post, a professor of preventative medicine and director of the Center for Medical Humanities, Compassionate Care, and Bioethics at Stony Brook University said:

> Rx: Help others. This little prescription has the side effect of benefiting the helper, so long as one does not become overwhelmed. Research in the field of health psychology, and all the great spiritual traditions, tells us that one of the best ways to get rid of anger or grief is to actively contribute to the lives of those around us. Science supports this assertion: giving help to others measurably reduces the giver's stress; improves health and

well-being in surprising and powerful ways; renews our optimism about what is possible; helps us connect to family, friends, place, and lots of amazing people; allows the deep profound joy of our humanity to flow through us and out into the world; and improves our sense of self-worth.

"Sure Sheryl, it worked for you, and this Post guy sounds lovely, but I still think your experience was a fluke."

I mentioned earlier that I used to work with the severely mentally ill at a Day Treatment facility. My clients were suffering from schizophrenia, bipolar disorder, multiple personality disorder, etc. I was tasked with working with the young adults (late teens to late 20's). Business as usual at the facility was a revolving schedule of classes based on: What is my disease? What are the symptoms of my disease? What are the medications used to treat my disease? What coping mechanisms can I use to feel better about my disease?

Are you noticing a pattern here? Two actually.

1) A strong focus on the actual disease

2) A victim mentality where the clients remained focused on themselves.

Any guesses as to whether anyone got better?

Here's the thing, I myself had tried dwelling in my sorrows for a while. It didn't make them go away. It didn't make them any easier to cope with. And it sure as hell didn't do anything to make anyone else's life better. It wasn't until I "got over myself" and focused on fixing someone else's problems, that I was able to help my own situation. I began to wonder if my clients would benefit from some good old volunteering.

Thankfully my boss was open to the idea and we put together a trial program for the young adults. Compounding the power of volunteering with the therapeutic benefits of animals, we went to a local animal shelter and the clients were tasked with walking and socializing the animals for two hours, one day a week.

Let's get a bit science-y for a few minutes. These clients experienced hallucinations (they saw and heard things that weren't there) when they were at the mental health facility. Some of them had violent outbursts that were seemingly unprovoked. Others had severe social deficits and wouldn't speak to people around them.

Enter the pups. (That sounds like a great movie about dogs trained in martial arts — but I digress). During the six months that I accompanied the young adults to the animal shelter, we never once had a problem. That means that no one experienced any hallucinations or violent outbursts, and the socially inept clients conversed with the animals and shelter staff.

Ummm, whoa.

Did we enter some sort of magical vortex? Are animals really the coolest creatures on earth? (Okay that one is true — but not the reason for this phenomenon). I'm pretty sure I know what happened... these mentally ill clients finally got out of their own heads. Here's a breakdown:

1) They were given something else to focus on besides their illnesses.

2) They were given a reason for being. There's a reason that we identify with our jobs so strongly. We need to feel like we are contributing to the community. Even if we don't know it yet. A life without porpoise isn't much of a

life at all (I think I just created a Valentine's Day card for dolphins).

3) They were surrounded by people that they had something in common with (besides mental illness) and therefore felt that they belonged.

4) Added bonus here: they wanted to go on these "field trips" so badly that their behavior actually improved during the rest of the week. The opportunity to volunteer became positive reinforcement for good behavior.

Would you like to join me in a round of "Ummm, whoa"?

Brafman calls this "Meaning Making" in <u>Succeeding When You Are Supposed to Fail</u>. He talks about longitudinal (lasting for several years) studies that show how people who face adversity fare much better when they find meaning in life. This means using spirituality, having close interpersonal relationships (remember the Charlotte's Web of Emotional Support chapter?), or finding a cause you care about. Michael F. Steger, director of the Laboratory for the Study of Meaning and Quality of Life at Colorado State University says:

> What we've found is that there are two ways of creating a meaningful life. One way is to surround yourself with meaningfulness in your life, whether it's through close family ties, volunteering your time and knowledge, or finding a career that's a calling. But even if your current work is not exactly your passion, focus on anything in your life that engages and inspires you: cooking a special meal, going on a bike ride, catching up with an old friend, singing or playing music, making a difference in someone's life. We tend to forget about the power of all the little things that bring meaning into our life.

I lean towards the making a difference in someone else's life because then you get to make your life better AND someone else's. Back to feeding two birds with one scone.

How can you make this work in your life?

Volunteer. Or at the very least, do something nice for someone else. Help an old lady put groceries in her car, send a Just Thinking of You card to someone who might be a bit down.

Okay, maybe there is a bit more to it than that. First, I want you to think about what you would do if money was not an issue. Imagine for a moment that you have all of the money that you, your family, your close friends, and anyone else you care to support, would ever need. Any decisions you make going forward will come entirely from a place of love. All of your needs are taken care of. Go ahead and bask in that feeling for a moment. I'm going to as well......

Now, what do you want to spend your time doing? What will make you get out of bed in the morning?

If you just pictured yourself in a pile of pups with a kitten climbing to the top like the cherry on the cuddle sundae, get thee to an animal rescue.

If you want to share your love of reading with a child, you can volunteer to tutor or organize a book donation event for the less fortunate.

If you lost a loved one to a specific disease, you can raise awareness for the cause and money for research. Example: My now ex-boyfriend lost his father to prostate cancer and sported a 70's porn star moustache for Movember. He spent November raising money and awareness for prostate cancer research. I spent November counting down the days until December 1st when he could start growing back his sexy beard. Oh yeah, and I supported him, too.

Does it break your heart to see homeless people begging for money or food? Work with a local organization to serve them meals, collect toiletries, or build housing.

Did your grandpappy serve in the military? There are plenty of underserved veterans in this country that could use food, clothing, a ride to the doctor, or just a person to talk to.

Are you horrified by the trash bucket we've turned this planet into? Volunteer with some environmental organizations to do a beach cleanup or help reinforce hiking trails in the woods. Bonus: if you happen to be a single woman and you are in the market — there are some damn good-looking men volunteering to improve the environment. Single guys — get thee to an animal rescue. As long as you don't mind sharing a bed with 42 dogs and a few cats, you will have your pick of the litter (had to, sorry).

If you just fanned yourself like Scarlett O'Hara and are now officially taken aback because I keep mentioning the personal benefits of volunteering, stand by for a truth bomb.

Who cares if you get something out of "giving back"?

In eight years of volunteering with animals, I have never had a dog put his paws on his hips and say, "Excuse me, but you are getting way too much out of helping me. I'm going to need you to dial it back a bit so I can benefit more."

Doesn't. Happen.

Volunteering isn't a zero-sum game where if you get too much out of it, the beneficiary of your time gets less. In fact, would you rather have a happy, joyful person helping you out or a cranky, resentful bastard who'd like to be doing anything but?

So go ahead! Reap the warm fuzzies! Get the psychological benefits. Gain the work skills. Make the social connections. Get healthier. Hell, find your soul mate. The animals, children, people inflicted with disease, environment, etc. don't mind.

A 2010 survey of forty-five hundred American adults found the following:

- 89% reported that "Volunteering has improved my sense of well-being"

- 73% agreed that "Volunteering lowered my stress levels"

- 92% agreed that volunteering enriched their sense of purpose in life

- 72% characterized themselves as "optimistic" compared to 60% of non-volunteers

- 42% of volunteers reported a "very good" sense of meaning in their lives, compared to 28% of non-volunteers.

The Do Good Live Well survey was released by United Healthcare and VolunteerMatch. For more information, please visit www.Volunteermatch.org

Exercise

Thought you did that when you visualized yourself in a pile of puppies? Wrong! You actually have to go do something now.

Are you about to whine that you don't have any time? If you turned on your television in the last six months, you've got time.

Do you have children and no babysitter? Bring them with you. It's never too early to teach kids the power of doing for others.

No money? Yeah, I didn't have any either when I started. Guess what happened? I made connections, and one of them got me a job.

Take a good look at your schedule and carve out a few hours a week or a month to get involved. Like anything else that matters, put it on your calendar and make the commitment.

Whatever your cause, whatever your skills, whatever your time allotment, there is an organization and a population that needs your help. The best part is you need them, too.

Chapter 9

I'm Good Enough, I'm Smart Enough, And Gosh Darn It, People Like Me

A few years ago I reached into my backseat looking for something and had to push around dog food in Ziploc bags, a yoga mat, and a pair of hiking boots.

I'm not telling you this to suggest that I'm a slob. I'm telling you, because as I was rooting around in tangible representations of my passions and hobbies, I realized that I finally liked myself. I was pleased with who I had become and how I chose to spend my time. I loved my life.

To some, this may not seem like much of a feat. But when I was married, I wasn't happy. I was resigned. I was a good wife and daughter, an amazing puppy momma, a good worker, an okay human being, but I wasn't truly happy with my circumstances or myself.

Right now can you honestly say that you love who you are?

If you can, good for you! I wouldn't suggest skipping this chapter, but if you'd like to skim over parts, I won't be insulted.

If you can't say that you like yourself, you are not alone. And we've got some work to do!

The way I see it, most of the world's problems are due to a lack of self-esteem. I know, that's a huge sweeping statement and I'm gonna stick to it. In my own life, I can attribute all of my stupid decisions (and if I listed them here, this would become a <u>War and Peace</u>-length book and your eyes would fall out of your head), to a lack of self-esteem. If I had believed in myself more, if I had considered myself worthy of setting and maintaining boundaries, if I had had the confidence to pursue greatness rather than settling for mediocrity, let's just say life would be a tad different.

How about the rest of the world's problems like wars, greed, violence? When we dominate someone, when we lash out and try to hurt them, I believe it's just our inner child saying, "I don't feel good enough about myself, so I need to put you down in order to feel better." People that are truly happy with themselves don't need to hurt others. A lack of self-esteem is just fear. Fear of not being accepted. Fear of not having enough (fill in the blank here).

Am I just being naive, or is our biggest issue a lack of self love? One of the wisest philosophers of our time, Yoda, once said, "Fear is the path to the dark side. Fear leads to anger. Anger leads to hate. Hate leads to suffering."

Let's scale it back a bit. I'm not looking to create world peace with this book (although that would be pretty damn cool). Can you think of any decisions that you made, any dates you went on, any person you married, jobs you stayed in, emotional borders that you allowed to be breached all because you didn't believe that you deserved better?

Why don't you take a moment and make a list of your three dumbest decisions and see if you can't tie them back to low self-esteem.

a) What I wish I hadn't done:

b) Why I think I did it:

1a) _____

1b) _____

2a) _____

2b) _____

3a) _____

3b) _____

"I think you're wrong Sheryl. I made bad choices for totally different reasons!"

If you couldn't tie your actions (or lack thereof) back to self esteem, let's try a little six degrees of Kevin Bacon. Let me give you an example. I decided to devote six years of my life to a course of study that could only end in one place: the FBI. I did this because my mom thought it would be perfect for me. Wait. Did I? Or did I not have enough belief in myself to tell my mom, "I don't want to chase serial killers for a living. I want to teach people how to eat well and stay healthy"? Even when your first instinct is to attribute decisions to another reason, it probably still boils down to self-esteem, it will just take a few different layers, or some mention of Footloose to get there.

So let's assume that you have already accepted my hypothesis about the lack of self-esteem being the root of all that is evil in this world. What do we do about it?

First, we need to understand exactly what self-esteem is. Second, we need to figure out where we are out of alignment. Third, we need to make changes and get *into* alignment.

Easy peasy, right? Right.

Let's take a look at the Six Pillars of Self-Esteem, the work of Nathaniel Branden. He breaks self-esteem down into six characteristics that contribute to your level of "I love myself-itis" (my words, totally not his). Here are the pillars; I will go into some detail below.

1. The Practice of Living Consciously

2. The Practice of Self-Acceptance

3. The Practice of Self-Responsibility

4. The Practice of Self-Assertiveness

5. The Practice of Living Purposefully

6. The Practice of Personal Integrity

The Practice of Living Consciously

Do you ever find yourself answering soul-searching questions with "I don't know"?

What do you want to be when you grow up?

What does your ideal day look like?

What does your ideal mate look like?

If I could start a business, what would it be?

What's my life's purpose?

Drowning in a big sea of "I don't know"?

Branden posits that we actually have way more knowledge then we give ourselves credit for. He suggests that when we ask ourselves questions (he uses sentence completions), we activate hidden resources and are able to tap into that knowledge to make decisions.

We spend so much time keeping busy, being bombarded constantly by stimulation. Have you ever made dinner, music on, Bluetooth in your ear and talking to a friend all at once? Probably not much opportunity for listening to your inner voice.

Jedi Master Yoda said, "You will find only what you bring in."

While I'm no Jedi master, the way I see this is to stop asking your parents, friends, teachers, bosses, that guy that delivers the sandwiches on a tiny cart during lunch, and the mailman, to make your decisions for you. You have the knowledge you need, you just have to shut up for a minute and listen to it.

The Practice of Self-Acceptance

"Our deepest fear is not that we are inadequate. Our deepest fear is that we are powerful beyond measure. It is our light, not our darkness, that most frightens us."
– Marianne Williamson

Did you know that not only do some people seek to disown the "bad" parts of themselves, some even try to shirk away from the good parts? Yes. Believe it or not, some people are actually more afraid of their awesomeness than they are their suckiness. When you accept that you are awesome, you just might have to take the spotlight and let everyone see how awesome you are... and that's fricking terrifying!

Better to hide in the shadows, looking up through your eyelashes and repeating "Nothing to see here, just little ol' me."

NO IT'S NOT!!!!

Branden suggests that practicing self acceptance is one of the requirements for having good self-esteem. You must embrace the bad and the good parts of yourself. You can use whatever words you'd like, but here is a template:

I am not very good at_____ and I am amazing at _____.

Here's mine so you have an example:

I can't mail a birthday card on time to save my life, and my brownies will give you a glimpse into the divine.

or

I'm not very good at removing produce from my vehicle or purse before it rots, and I would do anything for my loved ones.

Accept yourself. You are the only self that you will ever have. If you don't like who you are, change it.

In the words of my favorite cartoon sailor: "I am what I am, and that's all that I am." - Popeye

The Practice of Self-Responsibility

Remember that whole chapter on never labeling yourself as a victim? Yep, that's what he is talking about here. You are responsible for your actions. You are responsible for your choices. You are responsible for your decisions. Accept that and embrace it real quick.

The Practice of Self-Assertiveness

Be real.

No, I'm not trying to sound all sassy here. The practice of self-assertiveness is literally being the real you. It means being authentic despite outer influences. (Greek lesson - "auth" is from the Greek prefix "auto" meaning one's self).

As a storyteller, I like comparing the word authentic to the word author. And boy, do I have a story for you.

A few years ago I had an experience that I'm still not ready to talk about (maybe someday), but it prompted me to write a novel about it. I came up with a character, put her in a similar situation (though much worse for her), and then sent her down a path that I would've taken if I had a monstrous set of balls. The book was pretty damn funny if I may say so myself. But I was having a slight problem finishing the story. It just seemed to be hanging, and no matter what I did, I couldn't figure out the ending. As many authors do, I turned to my trusty author friends to read and critique my book. Before I tell you what happened, let me assure you that I love the crap out of these friends. They are all brilliant writers, wonderful people, and supportive to boot. I am grateful to have them in my life and my writing skill wouldn't have gotten to where it currently is without their help. Back to my story.

I sent my novel out to my beta readers... and that's when shit got ugly.

With every email that came pouring in, I made a change.

"You write mystery. You should make this into a mystery." And so I did.

"Your main character should have more flaws." And so she got more flaws.

"You should introduce this character earlier on in the book." Meet the character.

"You should have another character that does..." More characters joined the cast.

I made every single change they suggested. Even when it didn't feel quite right. I made months worth of changes, altering every aspect of my book to fit the "suggestions" that I was given. And when I was done royally f-ing my book, I sent it to another friend. The grand poobah of critiquers. I didn't get an email back. He came over to deliver the news. Probably should've been my first sign.

We sat down in the living room, cups of tea in hand and my dog's tail wagging as she eagerly awaited the reviews. Then he laid it on me.

"Sheryl, the way I see it, there are two problems with this book. First, it's disjointed, schizophrenic almost. Your first draft may not have been fully fleshed out, but it made sense. This doesn't make sense anymore."

Akasha's tail slowed, and I gulped down my tea, wincing from the burning sensation in my throat.

"The second problem is that your main character is not the heroine of the story."

Akasha and I both cocked our heads to the side.

"Lauren (my main character) isn't making her own decisions. She's just going along with everything that her new best friend says. The best friend is actually the heroine of this story."

Well shit. My main character was a reflection of me. Her best friend was a reflection of my best friend at the time. Their relationship was very similar to ours. In essence, he had just told me that I was not the heroine of my own story. I was not the author of my own life.

Ouch.

Years of therapy and no one had ever so succinctly communicated that observation to me. Therapy bills aside, the worst part of this was that he was right. Remember how a few paragraphs above, I advised against asking the mailman for life advice? Yeah, I had been doing that for a really, really long time.

I had taken advice from so many people that I had completely destroyed my novel... what was I doing to my life?

I want you to think about the last few major decisions you've made. Maybe they were selecting a career path, choosing between two potential suitors, picking a vacation spot or a new car. Got some ideas in your head? Good. Did you make those decisions or did you allow someone else to impose their will on you? Notice that I said *did you allow* instead of *did someone impose* — that's taking responsibility for your decisions and not being a victim.

Our responsibility in this world is to bring who we are into it. If our higher power, or the black hole that we crawled out of wanted there to be two of the same person, he (she, it, his noodley goodness) would have created carbon copies of the best of us (why am I thinking about Channing Tatum now?). You are meant to be you.

The Practice of Living Purposefully

> To live purposefully, Branden explains, is to use our powers for the attainment of goals we have selected: the goal of studying, of raising a family, of starting a new business, of solving a scientific problem, of building a vacation home, of sustaining a happy romantic relationship. It is our goals that lead us forward, that call on the exercise of our faculties, that energize our existence.

Crap. Did we just get into goal setting? If "goal" is just another four letter word to you, listen up. A very smart cat once said: "If you don't know where you are going, any road will get you there."

Did you ever pick a friend up around six PM and have the: "What do you want to have for dinner?" "I don't know, what do you want to have for dinner?" "No idea, let's just drive around until we find something that looks good." — conversation?

Let me guess. Did you end up grabbing Taco Bell drive-through at one AM because you couldn't decide on a cuisine until it was too late, so you ended up eating Chalupas with twelve packets of hot sauce in the front seat of the car and bitching about how you should've gotten sushi when it was still open?

We've all done it. If you don't know what your goals are, you won't achieve them. If you don't set a plan for your life, you will end up wandering aimlessly at one AM and eating food that you didn't really want to eat in the first place.

I'm going to go a step further with this living purposefully thing and remind you to find something greater than yourself to focus on. All of the goals that Branden mentions are important, but you should also have goals outside of your own tiny little world. I've already admitted that my goal isn't world peace (not that I wouldn't like it), but I still strive for something much greater than myself. I'm working towards a time when our animal shelters are there for the sole purpose of temporarily housing family pets who slipped out of the backyard and are just waiting for their parents to come pick them up. I'm working towards a day when no animal is homeless, abused, over-bred, or killed for "space."

What are your goals? What do you want for yourself socially? Professionally? Physically? For your family? For your friends? How about for the greater good?

The Practice of Personal Integrity

When I outlined this book, there were two words that I put down on my index card to get me started: "authenticity" and "integrity." I'm proud to say that this was before I began studying Branden's book, so I was already on the right track!

"Integrity is the integration of ideals, convictions, standards, beliefs — and behavior," writes Branden. "When our behavior is congruent with our professed values, when ideals and practice match up, we have integrity."

How do you feel when you say that you are going to do something and don't? How do you feel when you are very clear about your morals in a certain regard, but go against them for some reason? I'm guessing not so warm and fuzzy.

Have you ever professed not to talk about people behind their back and then slurped down some juicy gossip? Have you ever sworn off drinking after making a complete ass of yourself in front of your boss, only to reconnect with a vodka bottle the very next night?

Right now I'm picturing one of those after-school specials from the 80s. There's a group of teenage boys torturing a classmate. Most of them are really into it, poking fun (both figuratively and literally) at the smaller kid, but one of them is standing back, battling guilt. He knows it's not right to bully people, and he knows that he should stop it. But he doesn't. His behavior is out of alignment with his beliefs. He's going home in a really bad mood today.

When our behavior is out of alignment with our beliefs or when we break a promise to someone (or ourselves), we are chipping away at our self-esteem. We are sending the message to our subconscious that we are no good and can't be trusted. I don't know about you, but I don't want to hear that message from anyone, especially myself.

I've heard integrity described as "doing the right thing, even when no one else is watching."

I've got bad news for you: someone is always watching. And it's you.

If you don't already know what your beliefs are — perhaps you've been living so long with someone else's — take some time to figure out what *your* moral code is and then stick with it. You will have a lot more respect for yourself when you do.

Exercise

I had two more words written down on that index card that I haven't yet mentioned: "Lies Bag." Let me tell you a quick story before you get to work.

My parents divorced when I was four years old, and my mom and I went to live with my grandparents. My grandfather was a loving, warm, good-hearted man who loved his family unconditionally.

My grandmother… wasn't. We'll just leave it at that.

I would go visit my father one night a week and every other weekend. And when I got home, my grandmother would lead me through a "ritual" if you will. It was called the Lies Bag. It was a paper bag from Barnes and Noble with the image of a great author on the front and the words "Lies Bag" written in black Magic Marker across the top. It was kept in the pantry closet beside the cereal and larger bulk items.

I would come home and she would make me tell her everything that my father said, then I would have to discount it as a lie and ceremoniously throw it into the bag. (If you are looking to truly screw up your children, I highly suggest employing this method.)

All kidding aside, this was a horrendous practice that no child should ever be subjected to, but what if we can use it now? What if we can take some good from it and use it to improve our self-esteem?

Here is your exercise:

Decorate a bag, a box, a trash can or whatever, with the word "Lies" and whatever else you'd like to put on it (may I suggest a glittery skull and cross bones?). Now, I want you to think of all the bullshit you've taken in over the years. From your mom's very first, "You shouldn't eat that, you'll get fat," to your grade school teacher's, "You'll never amount to anything," to your boss's, "There are 100 people waiting to take your job." Take that shit and throw it into the bag!

While you are at it, you know all that self-talk that you've got? Is it about your weight? Your ability to braise a pot roast? Your lack of social skills? Your inability to get ahead in life? I don't know what's going on in your head (I'm too busy listening to my own), but whatever you are saying to yourself... chances are that it's bullshit and you need to throw it into the Lies bag.

You might be one of those people that like fire. That's cool. Once you've done this, light that little bastard on fire (preferably in a BBQ, fire pit, or sink — and make sure there is a fire extinguisher nearby. You won't feel very good about yourself if you burn the house down).

The important thing — besides not burning everything down — is that you keep up with this. We are constantly bombarded with messages (ahem... lies) from the outside world. You should do this every so often to clean out the bullshit.

Chapter 10

Grab Fear by the Balls

or

(The Diaper List)

I couldn't decide what to name this chapter, so I decide to use both of them. Obviously we are going to talk about fear (I will explain the Diaper List in a little bit).

Is fear ruling your life? Are there things that you haven't attempted because you are afraid of failing? Of looking foolish? Welcome to the club. Fear keeps us up at night. It prevents us from living the best life possible. It's like a little gremlin sent to screw with our happiness.

As far as I'm concerned, there are two types of fear, and I don't mean specific phobias such as xenophobia (the fear of strangers) or anatadeophobia (the fear that somewhere, somehow, a duck is watching you). I'm talking about two categories of fear: useful and not.

Some call it physical fear vs psychological fear. Tomato, tomato (well, that doesn't work as well in writing, does it?).

So what is useful, or physical, fear? Well, that's the fear that allows us to survive as a species. It's primal and innate. This fear keeps us from cuddling sharks — most of us anyway — it prevents us from wandering around in the dark when we are camping near a canyon, it makes us fear clowns (let's be honest, clowns are creepy as shit and we should avoid them at all costs). These fears are perfectly reasonable, safety-based, and necessary for humans to go on living (especially the clown one — seriously, who thought that makeup was a good idea?). This is where our fight vs. flight comes in: We are biologically programmed to know when to stand up for ourselves and when to run like a track star. Just in case you take things a tad too literally, when I suggest that you grab fear by the balls, I don't mean sharks (to be clear you should neither cuddle sharks nor grab them by the balls. Wait... do sharks have balls?)

Karl Albrecht, PhD talks about the five fears that we all share. I'm only going to list the first three for right now, because those fall under the "useful to our survival" category.

1) Extinction - beyond the fear of death, this is the fear of ceasing to exist.

2) Mutilation - fearing the loss of a body part (I'm pretty wigged about ever losing my eyes.).

3) Loss of autonomy - fear of being paralyzed or entrapped. A loss of control or freedom.

Carry on with your smart self by not walking down dark alleys in the middle of the night, dodging cars for shits and giggles (doesn't count if you are trying to rescue a dog), or peeing on electric fences. Adrenaline junkies take note, there are other ways to get that high, ways that aren't stupid.

So, let's get to the types of fear that we should grasp by the gonads and squeeze with all of our might. Psychological fear, or in my world — the not useful kind. The last two types of psychological fear that Albrecht discusses are:

4) Separation - fear of abandonment or rejection, loss of connectedness. (I might even argue that this should be rolled into # 5.)

5) Ego-death — fear of humiliation shame, or anything else that threatens our constructed sense of self-worth.

I need to give you a little background just in case you never rocked a PSY 101 class in college. There was this guy named Freud (father of psychology, was pretty sure that everyone wanted to have sex with their parents, saw a phallic symbol everywhere he looked). He wasn't my favorite star in the cast of characters that was early psychology, but he made some good points. He talked about the three parts of the subconscious: the Id, the Ego, and the Superego. For ease of explanation, the Id is the part that wants ice cream and will do anything it can to get it. The Superego is your mom's voice inside your head that tells you not to eat ice cream for breakfast because you will get fat. And the Ego is the middle man. He's the brain between the devil on one shoulder and the angel on the other.

Once you enter self-help land (filled with Unicorns spouting "I am" statements and sugar-plum fairies sprinkling gratitude glitter on your head), the Ego becomes a slightly different animal (not a unicorn though, sorry). The Ego is your sense of self, the construct of "me" that you have created. And the Ego is stubborn as shit. It doesn't like change, self improvement, or long walks on the beach. The Ego will do anything and everything in its power to maintain who it believes you to be. When you pump yourself up to ask for a raise and then stop dead in your tracks right outside the boss's office door, that's your Ego screaming loud and proud "You can't do that! We do not deserve a raise!." Ego puts on a brave face but it's actually just a frightened puppy cowering and peeing itself in the corner. (Excuse me, but I need to go give my dog a hug.)

To be fair, the Ego is kind of a dick. It's that voice that says "You can't diet. We are fat. That's all we will ever be." The Ego constantly reminds us of who we think we are (even though we are much more), and denies our ability to be anything else. Our Ego needs to go suck it.

So what do we do about it? Can we get an Ego-ectomy? That would be awesome, but as far as I know (and remember that I am not a doctor), there is not an Ego gland in the body that can be easily excised. What we *can* do is silence our Ego. We can pat it on the head and repeat "There, there. Everything is okay. You can take the night off. I'm going to go be awesome now."

I've found myself on multiple occasions facing down fear and mumbling to myself, "shut up, Ego. I've got this."

Does that make sense? Would it help if you pictured a green, slimy gremlin wearing a top hat and a monocle? That's your Ego. Or I may have just described the alien from Spaceballs. Whatever, you get the point.

Let's get back to fear. Just like the shit we talked about in the Introduction, fear happens. If you aren't afraid of anything, you either have a death wish, or you might just be dumb (sorry, but it's true). But if we live in fear, if we allow it to control who we are, what we do, how we live... that's a tragedy.

We must grab fear by the balls (or if you'd like to be a little bit more fluffy bunny about the whole thing, you are welcome to just embrace fear. Choose your level of badassery). How, you ask? There are a few different ways, but before we get to those, we need to identify what exactly your fear is and where it is coming from. In order to do this, we are going to incorporate some schoolyard interviewing.

Do you remember when you were a kid (or even more infuriating, an adult dealing with a kid), and you told a child to do something? What was the kid's response?

Why?

Here is an example:

You: I need you to clean your room.

Child: Why?

You: Because we are having company tomorrow.

Child: Why?

You: (getting increasingly annoyed) Because it is your Aunt Em's birthday.

Child: Why?

You: (about ready to bury the child in their pile of dirty clothes) Because she was born on this day 50 years ago.

Child: Why?

At this point, you have either thrown something across the room, or the conversation has devolved into the birds and the bees and you are now praying for some sort of natural disaster to blow through your house and distract everyone.

As irritating as it can be when talking to a child, this *Why?* technique can be used to get to the root of your fears. And it's super easy. Just keep asking yourself, "Why?." Here is an example to get you started (and I only wish I were kidding).

I am afraid of manatees. (Normally fear of an animal would be categorized under "life-threatening," except when it is irrational, ridiculous, and you are talking about the most peaceful creature on the planet.) So I ask myself: Why?

Because I had a nightmare once that one was driving a car and chasing after me. Why?

Because the manatee represents my grandmother and I'm still working to undo the psychological damage that she did. Sometimes I'm afraid that it's still chasing me and affecting my life.

Easy, right? Good. Now you try it. Yes, this is a bonus exercise. Try to contain your excitement.

I am afraid of _____.
Why?

Because _____.
Why?

Because _____.
Why?

Because _____.
Why?

Because _____.
Why?

Use some scrap paper if you need to keep going.

Chances are that you will discover that your "fear" isn't actually a fear. It's just a manifestation of a larger issue that you haven't dealt with yet.

In case you were wondering, it's perfectly normal to not only fear failure, but also success. It seems silly, why would you ever be afraid of achieving your dreams? There are a couple of possibilities.

1) Please read the following statement with a *Scarface* accent: Say hello to your little friend... the Ego. Your Ego believes you to be a failure. If you prove it wrong, it will spin around spitting pea soup and then melt into the floor. Perhaps your fear of success is less about others' perception of you and more about your own. If you haven't yet conquered your self-esteem challenges yet, you may not believe that you deserve to succeed. You might not feel yourself worthy of living your best life possible. Did that statement just perk up something deep inside you? Head back to the self-esteem chapter, "I'm Good Enough, I'm Smart Enough, and Gosh Darn It, People Like Me," if that resonated.

2) If you succeed, you become an amazing entrepreneur, a star on Broadway, the most adored philanthropist to ever grace our planet — your friends and family might not love it. Don't read that wrong, they still love you. But your ability to go after your dreams only reminds them of their inability to do so. You squashing your Ego and spilling green Ego juice all over the Persian rug in the living room will only serve to make their Ego stronger. When a loved one makes a snide comment about your aspirations, that's just their Ego. Don't take it to heart.

3) And maybe, you are just afraid that success will then lead to failure. You will be opening yourself to criticism, scrutiny, pressure, a more challenging life, handling the adoration of millions. It's a reasonable fear. Just look at a musician or actress that becomes a household name before they finish puberty. But just because you might fail (after you've already succeeded) is not a good reason to avoid putting yourself out there.

So how do we face our fear, embrace our fear, molest our fear? Just do it. (I hope I don't get sued by a sneaker company.)

What? Just do it? What kind of dumbass advice is that?

When I was 16, I went to the DMV and got my driver's permit. My mom took me to the Sunrise Mall at five o'clock in the morning and we switched seats. I drove around the parking lot about a million times, waving at the parked security guard each time we passed before I graduated to streets with actual cars on them. Looking back, it was actually a very good experience. Scary, but good. I was pretty excited to drive, so I wasn't a nervous Nellie behind the wheel. Until, that is, parkway day (that would be a freeway for you West Coast-raised folks). I was terrified. The thought of having to merge onto a road where cars zipped by at a minimum of 55 miles per hour made me want to hide under my dinosaur blanket and resign myself to public transportation.

My mom didn't make me do it. I told her I was scared and she said okay, and we went back to parallel parking, which after twenty years of driving, I've finally learned how to do.

Now Sheryl, didn't you say that this chapter was about embracing your fear, not Kow-Towing to it?

I'm getting to that. That day, she told me I didn't have to get on the parkway. The very next day, I did. She gave me the space to feel my fear, and then she forced me to conquer it. Boy, am I glad she did! Every time I jump in the car and head on a road trip, I'm grateful that I overcame that fear.

So yeah, just do it. I've got a sticker on my corkboard that says "Action Cures Fear." I do not have any stickers that say, "Thinking about stuff forever cures fear" or "Just hang on to fear; you'll be glad you did." You can talk about your fears all you want, but until you take action, they are there to stay.

Think you can't do it? Bullshit. Raise your hand if you are afraid of public speaking (did I get you again?). Does the thought of standing in front of a group of people make your heart do the cha cha, your palms dampen, and a bead of sweat roll down your forehead?

I used to be terrified. Yup, madam motivational speaker used to be afraid of public speaking. Not, "oh I wish those butterflies would calm down a bit" afraid. I was, "I'd much rather be swept away by a tidal wave of angry sharks than have to stand up and introduce myself in a room with more than two people" afraid. In case that doesn't paint a good enough picture of my terror for you, I had to present a paper in graduate school. I just had to read it, not even memorize or ad lib anything. I should've known there was trouble when my voice cracked while I was practicing ALONE IN MY ROOM. The next day, I got up to the front of the classroom, opened my mouth to start reading and nothing came out. Not a word, not a whistle, not a Beaker-like "meep meep." Nothing. I reached for a bottle of water and realizing that mine was still at my desk, I grabbed someone else's. Not a friend. Not someone I knew. I just saw water and was pretty sure that I would die without it.

Now, fear of public speaking is not a physical fear. No one has ever died from speaking in front of a group (although my smartass friend told me that someone did die of a heart attack on stage. I'm going to chock that up to bad genes and too many cheeseburgers and say that the actual speaking had nothing to do with it.) So, if we can't die from it, then it must be that damn slimy gremlin, the Ego, trying to preserve our sense of self (and that sense of self appears to be a wuss).

So, what happened between my graduate school disaster and now?

I joined my first writing group in 2009 and was asked to fill the Critique Group Organizer position. I jumped at the chance. Until I found out that I had to speak in front of the group every month. I remembered that feeling from college, the dread. But I knew that I had to do this. I had to tell the gremlin to take a hike. The president introduced me to Toastmasters and my life changed forever. I showed up to my first meeting and was surrounded by a supportive group that wouldn't allow me to be paralyzed by fear. By the end of the hour-long meeting, I had agreed to enter a Tall Tales contest. Yeah, my first speech was actually a contest. I wrote it, I practiced it, I nearly had a heart attack walking up to the stage... but I won. I was scared, but I did it anyway, and I'm so glad that I did!

What have you been putting off doing because of fear? Have you always dreamed of traveling abroad alone? Would you love to start your own business and tell your boss to take a flying leap? Is there a room full of your paintings that should probably be in a gallery somewhere instead of gathering dust?

Life (like clowns) is scary as shit. I can't tell you how many times I've sat down at my computer to work on my business, typing with one hand and checking my racing pulse with the other. I'd love to tell you that fear goes away, but if it does, I haven't experienced that yet. I still get a little scared every time I stand up in front of a room full of people, but you know what scares me even more?

Not standing up to speak.

How are you going to feel tomorrow if you don't go for it? How will you feel next month? Next year? How will you feel when you are lying on your death bed (I've always found this statement rather odd... like they roll in a special bed for you to die on. Perhaps this could be a new product line for one of the mattress companies. "Allow us to introduce you to the Morbid 2000. It's good enough to die on!")

Sorry about that. I got squirreled.

How are you going to feel if you use up your time here on Earth and never even attempt your dreams?

I call this the "regret hangover." Let me share where it came from.

As previously mentioned, when I moved out to Vegas I was in a bad way. Divorce, oncoming depression, and did I mention that my stepmom was in the hospital and then a rehab facility for about three months? Yeah, not the highlight year of my life. A good friend from high school called me and said that he and his father were doing a trip to Moab, Utah. They'd been talking about me and thought that I could use some time away from real life, connecting with nature.

I felt guilty leaving my parents during a health crisis but they assured me that it would be best for me if I went (not sure why they wanted me to go so badly. I was such a pleasure to be around back then). So, I packed up the small excuse that I had for hiking equipment, hopped into my Corolla (moment of silence for Caroline) and drove seven hours from Vegas to Moab, Utah.

It was dark when I arrived, so my friend met me at the gates to the campground and led me to the site. There were no lights except the moon, so he stuck close and prevented me from falling off the huge cliff that was right next to the bathroom (remember that evolutionary fear about not wandering into canyons in the dark?). The next day we headed out to our first hiking trailhead.

Now, let me give you a little background on my childhood experiences with hiking and camping. I didn't have any. My mom likes to joke that her idea of "camping" is a Howard Johnson. My father is deathly afraid of spiders and cleans his hands on the hour with wipes that he buys in bulk, and while my stepmom likes the outdoors, she has always had health problems that prevent her from doing active stuff.

But I did my best. I layered my clothes, put on my best sneakers, grabbed a backpack from my dad and wandered out into the great outdoors. Needless to say that without my friend and his father, I would not have wandered back in from the aforementioned great outdoors.

We hiked up the side of a mountain, the views getting more and more breathtaking with each step (as did the elevation for an unseasoned hiker). We hiked for hours, and I was pretty sure I would drop dead, but I kept going. Until we reached the very top. Well, not the *very* top. It was right before the very top when I tapped out. The last bit would require a rock scramble and finally a climb to the pinnacle. I... was done. My legs were weak, my arms felt like Jell-O, my heart was nearly racing out of my chest. I was deathly afraid of that climb.

My friend and his dad tried to coax me to take the last few steps, but I flat out refused. That stupid little Ego gremlin in my head was telling me that I couldn't do it. And I listened. That is until his dad said something that still echoes in my head.

"If you don't come up here, you are going to regret it for the rest of your life."

Well shit. He wasn't wrong. When I look back at my life, it's not the things I've done that I regret the most (although I've got quite the impressive list), it's the things that I haven't done. It's the guys that I didn't talk to in High School (his name was Alex Birnbaum in case you are wondering), the trips I didn't take, the jobs I didn't leave when I should have, the college that I didn't go to. Did I want to add that to the list? And that is how the regret hangover was born. His father's hand appeared over the shelf that separated me from the top. I braced one foot on one rock, lifted my other foot onto another rock and grabbed his hand. The view from the top — unforgettable.

What's the summit of your personal mountain? Is it financial freedom? A healthy relationship? Having a child (or admitting to your parents or spouse that you don't want one)? What's keeping you from "the top"? If it's just fear, ask yourself if the fear of doing whatever it is, is worse than the fear of not. If you can't live with the fear hangover, get your ass moving.

Fear sucks. Regret sucks more.

At the beginning of this chapter, I promised to tell you what a Diaper List is. Now, everyone knows what a Bucket List is, right? If not, it was made popular by a Morgan Freeman and Jack Nicholson movie about two men dying of cancer who set out to "experience life" before they died. Ideally, you've already got a Bucket List and are actively working on it! If you've got a list longer than Santa's with things you want to do before you die, but you aren't actually doing any of those things, that won't work. Don't wait until you've got a terminal diagnosis to start living.

Never actually seen a Bucket List and curious what is on one? A few items from mine to give you an example:

1) Pet a penguin - done

2) Attend a yoga retreat - done

3) Learn Spanish - not yet done unless yelling "Yo soy un penguino" throughout Spain counts

4) Raise a puppy to be a service dog - To Do

5) Travel to Japan for a traditional tea ceremony - not done

Notice anything about these? They are all cool experiences (for me at least) but they don't involve fear, just embracing an opportunity. Welcome to the Diaper List. That, my friends, is a list of the things that when you think about them, you pretty much shit yourself (I do have a way with words, don't I?).

Starting your own business and forgoing a regular paycheck... pass the Pampers.

Delivering a keynote address to twenty thousand people... that pair of pants will never be the same.

Joining the Peace Corp and traveling to Uganda to build schools... fan me now, I'm gonna faint.

Auditioning for The Sound of Music at the local theater... that's the sound of burning your skivvies.

Okay, you don't literally have to poop yourself (but no judgment if you do). I'm just trying to be gross to make a point here and shake you out of your comfort zone. What are those things that truly frighten you, but you absolutely want to do? (Unless you want to be a clown. We don't need any more of those.)

Right now, I want you to make a list of at least ten things that scare the bejesus out of you. "I just don't know" isn't an acceptable answer. You shouldn't even have to think very hard. You just have to give yourself permission to admit it.

I'm not suggesting that you do anything physically dangerous or financially destructive. I'm suggesting that you face your fear of being amazing and just do it already!

Ready for your exercise? Hey! Get out from under the bed. You can't grab fear by the balls while you are hiding under a bed skirt.

Pick at least one, but no more than three items from your Diaper List... and do them.

Whaaaaaaat!?!?! Am I crazy? Yes, but listen to me anyway. Remember that the only way to conquer your fears is to do them anyway. Take a technique from Improv: "Yes... and."

Yes, I'm scared of leaving my abusive husband and being alone... and I'm going to do it anyway.

Yes, the thought of putting my art out there for the world to see and judge is terrifying... and I'm going to do it anyway.

Yes, my heart tries to escape from my chest every time I make a sales call... and I'm going to do it anyway.

Are you noticing the pattern?

Exercise

Try your own:

Yes, _____ and
_____.

Yes, _____ and
_____.

Yes, _____ and
_____.

If you just whipped out a piece of paper and started writing your resignation letter, slow down there, Speedy Gonzalez. Your Diaper List item might have a few steps to it. If starting your own business has moved over to your To-Do List, you may want to lay the groundwork and get some money coming in before you give your boss the finger. Just saying, it's a bit of a challenge to be creative and excited when you are worried about paying your rent. Trust me on this. I speak from experience.

Overcoming fear is both the most difficult, and the easiest thing that you can do. What are you going to "just do" today?

Chapter 11

Who do you *Really* Want to be?

Did you ever have a day so bad, so frustrating, so infuriating, that you've dreamed of faking your own death and starting over with a new life?

I have.

I was never a huge *Sex in the City* fan. In fact, I only watched one episode out of the entire series. The episode, however, stuck with me for over a decade. (Hmmm, maybe I should've watched a few more shows...)

Carrie said, "In New York you are always looking for a job, a boyfriend, or an apartment." I believe that she then went on to talk about balance. How you are fine as long as at least two of those "legs" were standing. It was when you were searching for two or more at a time, that you had a problem. Now, I don't really remember how this conversation went, but that's what I took away from it, so we are going to accept it as fact and move on.

So, taking out the specifics, our lives are okay as long as we have at least two of the three "legs" to our life stool: a job, a place to live, and a relationship. Sounds reasonable. That's why they say it's difficult to work on too many goals at one time, right?

I've never liked to pay too much attention to what "they" say.

When my husband showed his true colors, I ignored that piece of advice. Within a two-week period, I lost (or walked away from) my relationship, my job, and my home. My stool became a slab of wood. Everything I knew, including my vision of myself, went bye-bye.

That's what sucks so much about divorce — or any major loss of a relationship including death — or losing your job, or your abilities, etc. Of course there is sadness and other aspects that cause emotional pain, but the biggest problem is your loss of identity.

We talked in the last chapter about how the Ego has a set vision of who we are. When the old *you* is no longer viable, all hell breaks loose.

I just saw *Dr. Strange* last night. I'm not usually into sci-fi or fantasy stuff, but I highly recommend the film if you are going through any changes. I'll just share the premise of the movie, hopefully without giving away any spoilers. Basically, Dr. Strange is a world renowned surgeon who can reattach spinal cords, fix nerves, put bodies back together again. He could probably fix Humpty Dumpty... and he knows it. Strange is an arrogant asshole whose identity is tied to his career and who believes that he is better than everyone else. He lives in the amazing apartment, drives the amazing car, treats the people around him like shit. Until his car accident. Strange wakes up to find that there is horrendous neurological damage to his hands and the prognosis for his career is poor.

I will stop there because I don't want to ruin anything for you (however, I really do suggest you see it. The special effects are amazing, of course, but from a personal development standpoint, they rocked it. I was jotting down quotes in my phone throughout the whole movie). So Dr. Strange is pretty much pure Ego. His sense of self and his happiness is entirely related to his career. He is a surgeon. When he loses his sense of who he is, his world crumbles.

Have you ever experienced this? Are you experiencing it right now? Have you ever woken up a lawyer, CEO, line cook, nurse and then gone to sleep devoid of an identity?

When we tie who we are to what we do, we lose who we are when we can no longer do it.

Have you ever woken up happily married (you thought) and gone to bed lonely and waiting for the divorce papers to be drawn up?

Life changes in an instant, and we are often left clutching the remnants of our former life like a teddy bear that's been burned in a house fire.

A friend of mine is a martial artist, mediation teacher, an Ordained Buddhist, and a Daoist Priest. A few years ago, I took a beginner's meditation class with him. I sat on my tiny little cushion and prepared to learn how to fix all of my problems with meditation (go ahead and ask how that went). He started out the class with a question:

"Who are you?"

A few students tried to answer with their professions, student status, stay-at-home mom designation, but he shook his head. I thought I was being all Madam Smarty Pants and raised my hand. "I am Sheryl." He shook his head. There were a few more attempts: nationality, religion, hometown, hobbies, genus and species, etc. until finally he put us out of our misery.

"The answer is," and then he stopped talking.

The class nodded so as not to come across as daft. But no one knew what the hell he was talking, or rather *not* talking about.

"When you seek to identify yourself, you limit yourself."

Ohhhhh.....

That sort of clicked. If I *was* my job title, I couldn't be anything else. If I *was* my relationship status, I couldn't be anything else. Just a note of advice: While this practice is wonderful for life and meditation, and connection with your higher power or whatever, it does not work at networking events.

Them: "Hello, My name is Susie. I'm a personal trainer and massage therapist."

You: "Hello." Followed by silence and intense eye contact that makes Susie giggle nervously while pretending her phone is ringing even though it hasn't made any noise.

So back to identity. Yours has gone the way of the dodo. You are no longer a (insert your previous job title here). You are no longer married to (insert the name or the expletive you use to describe your ex here). You have lost the ability to (insert something that meant a whole lot to you here).

Well, what the hell do you do now?

If this was a physical loss, say your house burned down, would you go into what used to be your kitchen and start making dinner? Would you walk over to where your shower used to be and take your clothes off (not advisable: neighborhood watch might get upset... or very excited). Probably not. You might mourn the loss of your walls and all your possessions, but then you're going to go ahead and start rebuilding. You are going to hire some people to carry away the wreckage (let's call them divorce lawyers), and then you are going to put up a new house.

Ideally you've got really good insurance and a savings account that will allow you a place to stay while you rebuild, or at the very least a good friend (support system) that will let you crash on their couch during construction.

Let's start rebuilding your house! (I'm going to stop using the house metaphor now, lest you abandon this book to watch HGTV for the next month).

You have freedom. A freedom that can only be provided through loss. I know that sounds a little weird, but sometimes the hardest thing to do is to walk away from something that's "okay" or comfortable. Well, woohoo. The hardest part has been done for you. Now it's time to rock your new life. My friend had some pretty sage advice for me when I was freaking out about starting my own business after I had been laid off. "It's not like you are walking away from a $200k a year position. If this doesn't work, you're still making the same amount of money as you are right now." Ouch, but true. You are free to fail.

Let's take a look at some steps to guide you through your rebuild. It's important to be honest here. No one else is looking at this so if you lie, you are only hurting yourself. (Ugh, I sound like a second-grade teacher. Eyes on your own papers, kids!)

1) Who do you want to be? Do you want to meet Prince Charming and have the children that your ex never wanted? Or are you thinking it might be nice to rock the single life and travel the world? Do you want to go into a completely different industry, or maybe even start your own business?

A wise philosopher, Cantus Fraggle once said, "You could be whatever your little heart desires.

You could be a walkin', talkin', breathin' ball of fire."

Now there are a couple of questions that go with this.

a) What are your passions? What gets your heart to do the two-step? Do you love to travel? Does whipping up a soufflé make you feel like a goddess? Do you get a tingle of joy every time you balance a checkbook?

I do a little jig when I get to
_____.

b) What are your talents? What are you really freaking good at? Do you have a yen for connecting people? Are you a wiz with a wrench? Do friends comment on your ability to problem solve?

I am absolutely amazing at
_____.

c) What are your skills? Perhaps you weren't born with the ability to write, but you've learned how along the way. These aren't necessarily skills that you've learned at work, they could even just be life skills. Everything counts.

I've learned how to
_____
.

d) What do you suck at? Here's where it's important to be honest. If your passion is cooking, yet you've never met a chicken you couldn't burn, being a chef might not be a good career goal for you. That's not to say that you couldn't work really, really hard at it for the next forty years, attend culinary school and beg for tutelage from the most creative minds in the industry... but maybe there's something else you would love to do that would embrace your innate talents and put them to good work.

Things tend to blow up when I
_____.

2) Now that you've answered these questions, it's time to create a vision of what you want for your life. Be as specific as possible here. What do you want to do? Who do you want to be surrounded by? What does your perfect day look like? What are you wearing? How much money is in your bank account? What are you driving? Where do you live? What non-profit are you donating time or money to?

___

Okay, take a deep breath. I feel like I just interrogated you. You can now take the spotlight off and forego answering the, "Where were you on the 22nd of October?" question.

Exercise

I know half of this chapter has been exercises, but I'm going to give you one more to work on. Maybe you aren't embarking on a huge life change right now, and so you kind of breezed over the rebuilding questions in the chapter. That's cool. But just because you aren't experiencing that type of change now, doesn't mean that you never will. So I want you to do a little possibilities exercise to get the ol' juices flowing.

Fill in the blanks:

If I wasn't a _____, I would be a _____.

If I couldn't eat _____, I would eat _____.

If I didn't drive a _____, I would drive a _____.

If I didn't live in _____, I would live in _____.

You can make as many of these as you'd like. The point of it is to realize that life isn't a one-or-none kind of experience. I have a greeting card sitting next to my desk. There are two people laying in bed and an old, bearded man climbing in through the window. The text reads: When God closes a door, he opens a window.

Hopefully, you won't be as terrified of opportunity and possibility as that young couple who are watching an old guy break into their house.

Remember, even after you have rebuilt your life... there might be another fire. The less attachment you have to the "idea" of who you are, the better off you will be the next time your life goes up in flames.

Chapter 12

Everything Sucks...But Maybe?

I'm about to get a bit personal here (you know, as opposed to how guarded I've been with the rest of the book), so hold on to your pants.

Everything wasn't perfect in LALA land when I was married. Its imperfection didn't take away from the devastation of the loss, but I'd be lying if I said that everything was sunshine and roses. Look into the psychological issues as you will, but the truth is that we barely ever had sex. There had to be perfect planetary alignment, the tide had to be at a certain level, the temperature between 70 and 72 degrees, my body at its highest level of hormone production, and the Giants had to have just won the Super Bowl in order for us to have sex. I might be exaggerating that a little bit... actually, I'm probably not.

I assumed it was all me. When he came near me, let's just say that you could hear certain parts of my anatomy slamming shut. He was the first man I'd ever slept with, so I had nothing to compare the experience or my sex drive to. I'd always assumed that I'd enjoy activities in that department (I mean it looks like a lot of fun in movies), but while I was with him, I just resigned myself to the fact that I had the libido of a corpse.

During the divorce, I spent a great deal of my time trying to make sense of what had happened. Why me? What did I do to deserve this? Why did this happen? Most people don't like to accept that shit happens willy-nilly and for no apparent reason. We need to find meaning behind the craziness that is life.

A few weeks after my divorce, I was out on a date with a new beau (yeah, I didn't wait long — and no, I don't advise moving that quickly), and we headed back to his place. I won't get into specifics, and we didn't do the nasty, but things were getting pretty hot and heavy. And then I felt it. I felt my sex drive shift from Park to Drive, and my foot slide onto the gas pedal. Holy shit. I remember stopping to catch my breath and having a celebration in my head, fist pumping and all. I wasn't dead inside. I wouldn't continue through life with cobwebs growing in unfortunate places. This was the moment that I realized my divorce and all the pain associated with it had actually happened for a reason.

Now I'm not suggesting that getting my freak on was the only reason for my divorce. I believe that I wasn't exhibiting the fullest expression of my being while with him, and many more amazing things have sprouted because of that ending, but it all started with that one realization.

When you are in the thick of it, shielding your eyes from the piles of shit that the universe is heaping upon you, there is no more infuriating phrase than "everything happens for a reason." When your family or your friends or that damn coworker who works in the cubicle across from you and nods in agreement when you are on a personal call, says those five words to you... admit it, you want to beat them with a stapler.

So I apologize in advance (and will duck if any staplers fly my way) when I say:

Everything happens for a reason.

Don't hate me. I'm not trying to be trite. We may not always understand what's happening at the time. Years later, we still may not understand why the hell something happened, but there is a bigger picture at play here. Sometimes you have to clear out the old in order to make room for the new.

Let's use a driving analogy for a moment. Do you know when you are driving in that super thick fog where it looks like you can touch the air, and you can't see anything besides the tail lights of the car in front of you? Imagine for a moment, that there is someone or something floating around above the fog that knows exactly where you are going and will place, or clear obstacles from your path in order to get you to where you are supposed to go. You can't see it because there is a wall of fog surrounding you, but you aren't alone and your experiences, your pain, isn't for naught.

I'm not trying to preach here, just share what brings me comfort. Whether you consider that force God, the Universe, etc., it helps some people to know that there is a bigger picture that we won't necessarily see until we need to. I have a friend who doesn't believe in a higher power, and that's cool, too. However, when I ask her if she looks for meaning in hardship, she says no. "Things just happen because they happen." If that works for her, great. But that doesn't help me sleep at night.

Let's back away from the spiritual chat for now and just discuss finding meaning. Maybe you don't think that things happen for the greater good (lose a battle, win the war), but hopefully you can still learn some lessons from whatever experience you are going through.

A quick caution about doing this too quickly. It's important to go through the pity party stage first. It doesn't have to last long, but it has to happen. Feel your pain and don't try to rid yourself of healthy emotions. That will just drag out the recovery period.

Remember how I talked about losing my job in the Drowning Giraffe chapter? Yes, I embraced the possibilities that my new life had to offer, and this is a great and a wonderful way to look for meaning... just not yet. It was about thirty minutes post-layoff and I was already making plans for the future. I rushed into my recovery even faster than I'd rushed into dating after my divorce, not giving myself time (in either case) to process my feelings and mourn my loss. And it worked about as well as my first relationship. Six months into my "new life," I was breaking down and unable to move forward.

Okay, I don't know if that counts as a "quick" caution, but it had to be said. Now let's get back to how you deal with the slingshot full of poop that just came flying your way.

Let's start with some questions to get your opportunity river flowing.

1) What can I learn from this experience, and how can I change from it?

Did things with the "bad boy" you were dating blow up in your face... again? Did you learn anything about dating that type? Perhaps you should be looking for a nice guy (you know, with a job and manners) next time around? I sucked at History, but as George Santayana once said: "Those who cannot remember the past are condemned to repeat it." You don't just have to remember the past, you have to learn from it too.

2) Are there any positives that might come out of this negative experience?

Was the spouse that left you keeping you from being your awesome self? Have you had unexplained respiratory problems since you started the job you've just been fired from? (I sound a bit like one of those lawyer commercials: "Call 1-800-Wesuetheirpantsoff.")

3) Did this experience happen to prevent a worse one from happening down the line?

Any time I hear that someone had a heart attack and lived, I have to think about this. A heart attack should be a huge ass wakeup call from the universe that you are doing shit wrong. You can ignore it, continue eating double cheeseburgers for three meals a day and driving to the mailbox at the end of your driveway, and eventually have a heart attack from which you do not survive; or, you can start eating right and exercising, releasing the extra 200 pounds you were lugging around, and learning to manage your stress, and live a long, healthy life surrounded by family and friends.

4) How can this experience make me a stronger person?

I like to look at scars (both physical and emotional) as a badge of honor. It means that you survived something. It's proof that you faced a dragon and came out the victor, and you can use that in your future endeavors. There's nothing more badass than facing a situation and being able to say "You think that's going to hurt me? I've faced way worse shit in my day."

5) How will this negative experience affect the course of my life?

Did you used to wake up every morning dreading going into work? Did you spend your days trying to keep your skin from crawling off you every time your sleazy boss called you into his office? Did you sit through meetings and pray that a fire would break out and engulf everything in its wake? Then one day, Mr. Sleaze called you into his office and fired you. You then went home and spent the next six weeks in a deep depression (and the same dirty-ass pajamas) eating ice cream by the truckload and snacking on Cheetos that you found in the hood of your sweatshirt.

Ummmm... why? Clearly you were miserable. Being fired just gave you permission to change paths and find a new career that you are *meant* to do. Call it a course correction, if you will.

6) How can this negative experience affect the course of someone else's life?

Yeah, this one sounds a little bit weird, but remember that I set up my tent in the "Do Something for Others" camp. A few examples:

- the founder of Canine Assistants was diagnosed with MS. Instead of curling into a little ball and letting the disease ravage her, she started an organization that provides trained service dogs (for free) to people with disabilities.

- the founder of the Dustin Shilcox Foundation (you get one guess on what his name is) was in a horrible accident that left him paralyzed from the mid-chest down. He could've become a bitter douchebag, but decided, instead, to start a foundation to raise awareness for spinal cord injuries and money to fund research.

- My friend Jeffrey returned home from his Navy experience with a severe case of PTSD. He could've gone further down the rabbit hole of mental illness, but instead, he embraced the healing power of music and now teaches drumming to children in underserved communities, veterans, individuals with mental illness, and the blind.

Exercise

Now believe me, I really do understand how difficult it is to see the good in a bad situation while you are going through it. That's why I don't want you to find the good in your current situation just yet. I want you to practice by finding the positives in experiences from your past. I want you to understand that as blind as we are in the moment, we can find good once we have passed through the experience.

Let me give you an example. A client of mine has spent the last three years of her life caring for her ill father. Her business has suffered, her social life has suffered, her relationships with her other family members have been strained, and her stress level has skyrocketed. A few months ago, her father finally passed. As with the loss of any loved one, she was incredibly upset and had to go through a mourning period. However, as the fog of her sadness began to lift, we were able to search for the good that came out of her father's passing.

1) She is now able to focus on rebuilding her business, servicing existing clients and attracting new ones.

2) Her relationship with her mother has become stronger.

3) She no longer feels bad about taking a day to pamper herself instead of being by his side.

4) She has started reconnecting with lost friends and making plans for her future.

On our last call, she happily reported that Thanksgiving was a joyful and peaceful experience. She's not happy that her father is gone, but the loss has freed her up to live her life again.

So what have you been through? Make a list of some of the most harrowing experiences of your life, and then come up with 3 (or more) wonderful things that have blossomed out of it.

The Bad	The Good (or the lesson)
_____	_____
_____	_____
_____	_____
_____	_____
_____	_____

You can keep going if you'd like, but whenever you feel like there is no hope, and no good that can possibly come out of a situation, reflect back on this exercise and find peace in the fact that something good will come from it.

Chapter 13

We Regret to Inform You That Your White Knight is Pending Administrative Review

Have you have spent most of your life waiting to find the teacher, therapist, relationship, coach, acupuncturist, past life regressionist, Zen Monk, Reiki Master (I think you get the point), who will make all of your problems go away? Someone who has the power to "fix" you.

Me too. When I moved out to Vegas after my divorce, I left no stone unturned. I was going to find someone who could tell me what was wrong with me, and then, fix it. Surely this exists, right?

Wrong.

Somewhere in between reading *It's Not Easy Being Green* (great book by the way, I highly recommend it) and visiting my umpteenth therapist, a friend said something very important to me... "There is no white knight coming to save you."

Well crap. You mean I'm going to have to do this myself? Yes, and also no. Let me give you a short explanation and then we will get into the meat of it (or the thick part of the tofu for the vegans out there).

Yes

Have you ever tried to help someone that doesn't want to be helped? Have you ever tried to keep (insert drug of choice) away from an addict or given career advice to someone who's quite happy perfecting the ass groove on their couch? It doesn't work. You can offer support, guidance, a ride to the methadone clinic, but until they make the decision to change, your actions ain't gonna do squat.

No

Who the hell told you that you needed to be fixed? You send those a-holes over to me. Why are we all walking around feeling so fricking broken? I've got some thoughts that I will elaborate on later.

Here's the meat:

Yes

Okay, we are back to why you have to do this yourself. Remember how we talked about not labeling yourself as a victim because it takes away your power to make a change? You know what happens if you label *someone else* your hero? The same exact thing.

A quick story (we were due for one, right?):

As I mentioned, a few years ago I was merely a shell of who I am today. I was scared, shy, self-conscious, embarrassed to introduce myself, etc. So I went to Toastmasters "TM". My TM family nurtured me, pushed me out of my comfort zone, volunteered me for leadership positions, provided a safe place for me to fail, and became my cheering squad. And so, for the last four years, I have been walking around saying "I owe who I am today to Toastmasters."

Welllllll.... that's not quite right. While they provided me with support, knowledge, and encouragement, I couldn't have done it without me. That's right, I owe who I am today to myself and my willingness to be led on a journey (not to mention working my ass off along the way). Now, please understand that I'm not suggesting you jump off your couch and start calling up your friends, family, and professional supports screaming "You bastards think that you made me awesome! I don't need any of you!" and laughing maniacally while deleting phone numbers from your contact list.

Humility and gratitude are necessary qualities in all human beings (I bet you know a few people who are missing those qualities and you probably don't like them very much). If you shouldn't give someone all the blame for hurting you, why would you give someone else all the credit for helping you?

When you accept that your white knight isn't coming, it gives you a certain level of responsibility for your happiness. And as we know, responsibility is scary as shit (like clowns). But it's also a blessing. Having the responsibility means that you also have the power. You don't have to spend every day examining your split ends and waiting for the prince to come and get you out of that tower. You get to choose precisely when you whip up a French braid, tie the end to a well-attached tapestry, and climb down to safety.

Welcome to self empowerment.

You may meet some squirrels on the climb down who offer to un-snag your dress from a rogue branch, a delightful blue bird who keeps you motivated and tells you Chicken Crossing the Road jokes on your way down, but it's still going to be you doing the rappelling. (In case you missed the metaphor and/or are afraid of squirrels, those are the people along the way that help you on your journey.)

There is an old adage in the speaking community about "not being the hero of your story." You should always have someone who helped you grow and solved your crisis. I understand where that comes from when you are relating your life story for someone else to learn. But I call phooey when it comes to actually living your life. You must be the hero of your own life.

Don't allow anyone to tell you that you aren't the most powerful person in your own life. When you do, you fall prey to being the sidekick in your own story. You are strong, you are powerful, and to bring us to our next point... you are fine just the way you are.

No

So how am I going to follow up that resounding "Yes" with a "No"?

I mentioned that we are all walking around wondering why we are so broken. And yes, everyone is. I went to a seminar once where they had us all close our eyes and then raise our hands if we battled with self-esteem issues. Then they had us keep our hands raised but open our eyes. Guess how many hands were up?

Every fricking hand.

So, if you ever meet a person who tells you that they have all the self-esteem in the world and have never battled with their self worth or doubted their ability to succeed... they are lying. Kick them in the shins and run in the other direction.

Why do you think we all feel like this? Well, I've got a couple of theories. The first is going to sound like a bit of a rant (as opposed to the rest of this book). I blame our materialistic society.

I said it. Have you ever looked up the statistics on advertising? I have and it's freaking terrifying. I found a study that said that the average adult, through television, radio, print media, and internet usage, is exposed to...

(Are you sitting down? If not, you probably should be.)

The average adult is exposed to 360 advertisements each day. What the what!?! Let me just whip out my handy-dandy calculator right now. Let's assume that the average person is awake for sixteen hours out of the day, and likely tied to one of the aforementioned sources of communication during those hours. That means that for every hour your eyes are open, you are experiencing 22 messages telling you that you need something you don't have in order to be a better version of you.

What are advertisements? They are little messages that tell you that the only way for you to be a: good person, attractive, a good parent, intelligent, respected by your peers, etc., is to buy their product. The thing is — even though they don't actually come out and say it — there's an assumption that you must make in order to buy into their game: YOU AREN'T ALREADY.

If you believed that you were inherently beautiful and a commercial for makeup came on, you would tilt your head back, swing your hair over your shoulder and let out a boisterous laugh. After all, you don't need chemical pigment to feel good about yourself. But there are probably only about five people walking around who think they are inherently beautiful, so the rest of us imagine how perfect our lives will be as soon as we head to the drugstore and pick up that lipstick.

Here's a quick little exercise for you. Every time you see a commercial or an ad in a magazine, take the product out of the equation and try and figure out what they are actually selling. Then ask yourself if buying similar products to fill that need has ever actually filled that need. Look at that, you not only get personal development advice from this book, you get money-saving tips as well.

I think there is another reason that we are all walking around feeling broken. It's because our parents feel the same way. If we do not love ourselves completely and we raise children, what do you think the likelihood is of those kids coming out loving themselves completely? I'm not trying to get all Freudian and "waaaahhhh, it's my mom's fault." I'm just trying to show you that we learn by seeing and hearing those around us. What messages did you get from your parents, and if you have a child, what messages are you giving them?

At least once a week now, my dad will do something and mumble to himself, "I'm so fricking stupid." I've picked up these messages for years and only during the last few have I been able to catch my own negative self-talk and gently nudge him not to speak that way to himself. I say, "Hey, don't talk about my dad that way." Be very careful of what you say to yourself. Remember, you are always listening.

I have a fellow speaker friend who tells a story of bathing-suit shopping with her (at the time) five-year-old daughter. She picked out a suit, helped her daughter into it and then sat back to delight in the utter cuteness. Until her daughter began to cry and said, "I'm so fat."

Five years old.

She had spent the past five years watching her mother struggle with her own body image. Five years of hearing that someone she believed to be perfect wasn't. And if mommy isn't perfect, how could she possibly be?

I bet you have your own experiences. If you were lucky, you picked up your insecurities from listening to your parents complain about themselves. If you weren't quite as lucky, you picked them up because those negative messages were given directly to you. Maybe your parents (or someone else) told you that you weren't pretty, or smart, or good at sports, or you'd never make anything of yourself.

Good news... those messages were actually still insecurities about the people who sent them; they were just disguised as complaints about you. Let's all join hands and rejoice in a round of "That's your shit!"

Now I'm not saying that you shouldn't strive to be better than you are. I'm certainly not saying not to work on self-development. If we aren't growing, we are dying. I'm saying that if we stopped looking at ourselves as broken machines that need to be fixed, and started thinking about ourselves as beautiful works of art that need to be fine-tuned, well, this would be a much better world.

There is a famous (though possibly incorrect quote) floating around by Michelangelo in reference to how he created his famous sculpture of David. "It is easy. You just chip away the stone that doesn't look like David."

Well, if he didn't say that, he should have. It's freaking brilliant. He didn't *create* anything, he just removed the garbage that didn't belong.

What if you are already an awesome, kickass being who accomplishes great things in this world? What if all you have to do is chip away all the crap that's preventing your true self from being seen?

Not an art person? Okay, look down. Do you have a super flat stomach? Do you think that when you do crunches and cardio, a six-pack fairy is going to swing by in the middle of the night and drop off your new sexy abs? (If you know something I don't, please send that fairy my way).

Nope. As you run, as you do your crunches, you are going to chip away at the fatty tissue that is covering up your real abs. (I hear there is something about not eating pasta too, but if it's between pasta and flat abs... well I never wanted to be a bikini model anyway.) You are already a masterpiece. Now it's time to remove the pieces that are covering it up.

I think, in part, this is why correcting your language to only include positive, active, in-the-now statements works. If you say, "I will have a million dollars in my bank account," it tells the universe that you don't have something, that you are imperfect. When you rephrase it as, "I have a million dollars in my bank account," you tell the universe that you are aware of your superb awesomeness and are just waiting for the rest of the world to catch up.

Exercise

Are you waiting for your white knight right now? (Say that five times fast!) What situation are you experiencing that you expect someone else to fix for you?

What are just a few action steps that you could take right now to resolve that problem on your own?

Chapter 14

The Platinum Rule

Remember in kindergarten when you snatched a doll away from little Susie and then proceeded to whack her on the head with it a few times before your teacher noticed? Then, Mrs. Whatever Her Name Was, took the doll from you, sat you down at your desk, and explained all about the Golden Rule: Treat Others as You Would Like to Be Treated.

Now this is a good rule, but honestly I've never been a huge fan of gold. I submit for your consideration....The Platinum Rule: Treat Yourself as You Would Like Others to Treat You.

Sheryl, why is this coming so late in the book? Shouldn't this be the first thing we practice?

Yeah, well (whistles quietly to herself) I just learned it, okay? Stop judging. Yeesh.

Last week I was reflecting on this past year with my mastermind group. It occurred to me that I hadn't accomplished quite as much as I'd hoped, and I settled myself in for some quality self-abuse. Until one of my partners stopped me dead in my tracks.

"It's been a rough year, Sheryl. Don't forget to practice kindness."

Well, I found this hysterical. Not because she said it in a faux-Austrian therapist voice, but because here I was writing a book on resilience and how to overcome setbacks and rock your life... and I forgot about being kind to myself. So it is three quarters into the first draft of this book that I finally sit down and reflect on kindness and self compassion as it relates to resilience.

Do you remember that scene in *The Da Vinci Code* where the pale guy takes out a whip and settles in for a nice evening of self-flagellation?

How many nights have you spent beating yourself up (no whip necessary)?

We hold ourselves to a different standard than we hold others to. We can call it a quest for self-actualization, a zest for self-development, or a yen for awesomeness, but we shouldn't. We should call it what it actually is: striving for an impossible goal of perfection. Now when was the last time you expected your spouse, child, employee, boss, friend, or your Chihuahua named Tex to be perfect?

I'm going to assume never, but let's take it a step further. If they turned out not to be perfect, would you then spend the rest of your life beating them up (either figuratively or literally) over it?

No! (If you said yes, you may be alone right now, and this may provide an indication as to why.) If someone you love proves to be flawed (as is the Human Condition) you would accept them for who they are, and maybe help them to become better.

So why the hell are we beating ourselves up!?!

"You, yourself, as much as anybody in the entire universe, deserve your love and affection." ~Buddha

According to Dr. Kristen Neff, self-compassion is similar to compassion towards others in that it involves recognizing suffering, feeling a desire to help end the suffering, offering kindness rather than judgment, and realizing that suffering, failure and imperfection is part of the human experience.

How many of us are really good at doing that for others, yet turn into Nazi drill sergeants when we speak to ourselves? (Raises hand)

Grab your carpet squares and your sippy cups, it's story time.

Earlier this year, I was driving to do my radio show. I got into the car, hopped onto the parkway, and was moving along when a rock came flying towards my windshield. Pretty sure that a rock that size would kill me, I jerked the wheel to the right to get out of the way. Well, maybe there was gravel on the road, or maybe my poor little Corolla just didn't like being jerked around like that. Either way, I lost control of the vehicle, swerving in and out of the lanes (thank goodness there was no one else on the road), before hitting the shoulder and flipping four times. I sailed through the air for what seemed like hours before coming to an upright position on the shoulder, facing the wrong direction. My side window was busted and my pants were covered in blood.

The first person at the scene was an off-duty fireman (ummm thank you, Universe) who kept me calm and still until emergency responders could arrive. He found my phone and called my parents to tell them what had happened, and even texted my co-host to let him know that I wouldn't be doing that show.

When the ambulance, fire truck, and heavy rescue got there, it was a whirlwind of activity. They cut my door off the hinges to get to me. When they found out that I was receiving chiropractic care for neck issues, they brought out the jaws of life, and cut the roof of my car off while a firefighter laid across me, protecting us both from the metal shards with a white sheet. I was removed from the car and brought to the ambulance where my parents peered in, tears streaming down their faces.

"I'm okay," I said, assuring them that I was going to live. At least, I was pretty sure.

If you've ever been through a severe physical trauma, you know that all self-consciousness, all self-esteem goes right out the window. EMTs', doctors, nurses, radiologists poked and prodded me. And thank goodness, I was alright. Partially at least. Maybe I wasn't doing so well at that exact moment, but I was going to be okay.

The doctor sent me home with staples in my head, stitches in my head and finger, a large gaping hole in my wrist, and a concussion. I was sore, sticky (dried blood is nasty) and shaken to my very core, but I was going to be okay.

This was a Tuesday. On Thursday, there was a meeting of my Women's Professional Council.

If a friend described that ordeal to you and then asked if she should attend a meeting two days later, would you ask her to pick you up a latte on her way to the meeting, or would you fashion her a suit made of bubble wrap and then barricade her into the house?

I went to the meeting. Against everyone's advice, with my parents doing everything besides physically restraining me, I went to the meeting. My ladies built a throne for me out of a roll-y desk chair and about 42 towels and blankets (we met at the animal rescue's adoption center). They all thought I was crazy.

Now I realize that I just wasn't being kind to myself. But I had to get moving! I had a business to work on, an empire to build, masses to inspire, and I think it was my week to go facilitate a lesson. The acupuncturist of the group cautioned me to "rest my brain" and allow the concussion to heal before I tried to push forward with my business. If I didn't give it time to heal, it would take even longer to return to my full-functioning self.

There was no time for resting, relaxation or convalescing! I had to get my ass in gear. And nothing anyone said to me was going to change that fact.

Would you like to guess how much I was able to accomplish over the next few months?

Grand prize if you said "Squat."

I couldn't focus, I had no memory, I was sensitive to sound and the occasional light pattern, my emotions were all over the place, and every time I laid down I went for a psychedelic ride that some people pay good money for.

By pushing myself and berating myself for not healing quicker than I did and not reaching my pre-accident goals, I actually made my recovery slower and wasted time in the long run.

The moral to what I now believe might've been an extremely long story: Practice self-compassion. Don't beat yourself up when you go through something difficult (actually don't ever beat yourself up).

So what exactly is self-compassion?

Dr. Neff breaks self-compassion down into three different categories:

1) Self-kindness vs. Self-judgment

2) Common Humanity vs. Isolation

3) Mindfulness vs. Over Identification

Let's take a look at each of these in some detail.

Self-kindness vs. Self-Judgment

Remember how we started this book? Shit happens. And a lot of times, shit happens because you did something maybe not so good.

That's okay.

We are going to make mistakes. We are going to fail to live up to our goals. If you wouldn't sit your best friend down in the corner and begin screaming, "You are fat, and ugly, and stupid, and you will never accomplish anything in this life because you are a worthless piece of poop," do not say it to yourself. Treat yourself with compassion and accept that you are not (and never will be) perfect.

Common Humanity vs. Isolation

Did you screw up today? Yeah, me too. Oh, and so did the other six billion or so people on this planet. Don't think that you've got the market cornered on screw ups. There is quite a bit of competition out there. It's good to feel special. We are all special. But we are not unique in our ability to make mistakes or exhibit weaknesses. You are also not the only one who woke up in a bad mood today. Suffering is another part of the human condition. In fact, suffering is so common that the Buddhists went ahead and created the Four Noble Truths all about suffering!

1) To Live Means to Suffer

2) The Root Cause of Suffering is Attachment

3) The Cessation of Suffering is Attainable

4) The Path to the Cessation of Suffering

I won't go into detail here, I just want to prove that you aren't inventing the wheel when you sit down to feel sorry about yourself and have a good cry.

Mindfulness vs. Over Identification

Let me simplify this one for you because it can sound a bit complex. In order to be compassionate towards yourself, you need to recognize and accept how you are feeling (no pretending not to hurt when you do), and then you need to use perspective (now where have we heard that before?) to place your experience on the grand scale of awesome to shit-tastic.

Here is a really harsh example: I feel sad because I lost my job; however, there are people dying right now because they don't have access to clean water. I should probably look for a new job and get on with my life as opposed to wallowing in depression. (The keyword here is "wallowing" — remember the five stages of grief.)

What happens when we self-flagellate?

1) As you saw in my car accident example, it actually took longer to heal because I wasn't kind and didn't give myself the space to convalesce.

2) I don't think anyone has ever had *improved* performance after being chewed out by a boss. Instead of telling yourself, "I suck, and I will never get any better," you can say, "I made a mistake and I am taking the necessary actions to correct it and avoid it in the future."

3) You may quit altogether. If you don't reach your goals, and then you beat the crap out of yourself for not reaching them, are you more or less likely to try again? I for one

would be trying to avoid that onslaught of "I suck-ery" that I know is headed my way.

4) When you abuse yourself, you give other people permission to do the same. Think about a family where the mother is constantly cutting down the father (or vice versa). After awhile, the children begin to show disrespect to the parent. They have been trained on how to behave. Same idea. You are constantly training those around you as to how you would like to be treated. You do this by setting (or not setting) boundaries ("You cheated on me once, and I forgave you — now you think you can do it again."), and by showing people how you treat yourself.

The Platinum Rule: Treat Yourself as You Would Like Others to Treat You

I always find the timing of the universe to be really hilarious. I was watching a comedy special with my parents last night (always dangerous... so much talk of sex that my dad and I can't make eye contact), approximately four hours after I wrote the beginning of this chapter.

My parents and I watched Iliza Schlesinger's *Confirmed Kills,* and besides being hilarious, it was also really timely. She was talking about feminism and how when we walk around calling each other sluts and whores, and when we use terms like "Walk of Sham,e" it devalues women and gives men the idea that they can do it, too. Yay for timing.

So you get it now, right? You understand why it is so important to practice kindness towards yourself. You now grasp how if you don't treat yourself nicely, no one else will either. And you are ready to hop on the back of kindness and ride off into the sunset together... right? Right.

But how do I do that?

Well, can we start off with how *not* to do that? If your idea of being kind to yourself is drinking yourself into oblivion or taking massive amounts of drugs or closing down a bakery because you ate all of the cupcakes, that is not being kind or self-compassionate. That's not to say that a celebratory (or consolatory) glass of wine isn't in order, or that you shouldn't bake up a batch of brownies after a breakup (but only bake half of them because you ate the rest of the batter). One evening of "well this sucked and a little something might make me feel better" is okay. It's when it stretches out into weeks or months and you find yourself at an AA meeting wondering where your life went wrong, that you have a problem. As I've mentioned before, have your pity party - just make sure that it doesn't turn into a prolonged fiesta.

So, now that we know what not to do, let's discuss what you should do. Kindness and self-compassion are all about nourishing your body and your soul. That means that you should be feeding your body healthy foods and giving it plenty of exercise and down time. Massages are a great way to thank your body and your brain for the beautiful work it is doing (and who can resist an hour of Enya). There is nothing wrong with treating yourself to the occasional spa treatment or a special movie or show (even if you just go by yourself). And I have found nothing more rejuvenative than time spent in nature.

This is all incredibly important, but there is something that is even more important: self-talk. We touched on it a little bit earlier, but it's worth discussing in more depth. What do you say when you talk to yourself? I want you to think about a time that you did something less than ideal. Maybe you went out with someone you shouldn't have or stayed in a relationship longer than was healthy. Maybe you screwed up a work project or failed to get a job that you had applied for. Take a few moments to get yourself into that state of mind and then jot down your inner dialogue. A few questions that might get your juices flowing:

1) What was your initial reaction to the disappointment?

_____

2) Did you call yourself any names?

_____

3) Did you characterize yourself by any of your behaviors (I did a stupid thing vs. I am stupid)?

_____

One of my favorite lines ever from a movie is in *Raising Helen*. Kate Hudson's sister passes away in a car accident and leaves her three children to live with Hudson, a single woman completely unprepared to raise children. On prom night, one of the kids goes to a motel with her boyfriend and Hudson and her other sister (Joan Cusack) show up at the motel to rescue the girl before she does something she will regret. Cusack busts down the door, gets in the teenage boy's face and says, "It's not that you are a bad person, it's just that you did a very, very bad thing."

One mistake, one poor choice, does not make or break us (most of the time); however, continued behavior eventually becomes our character.

The secret to being kind to yourself is to accept what has happened, continue to love yourself despite your foibles, and learn from the experience so that you can grow from it and avoid repeating the mistake. Super easy, right?

Maybe not that easy, but with practice, I think we can all get there. I walked up to my home office this morning carrying a cup of hot, raspberry hibiscus tea, a bottle of cold water (that I didn't want to tuck under my arm because of the chill), my cell phone, and my calendar. My dog was pacing me on the stairs.

Before I give away the ending, would you like to guess how well that turned out?

If you guessed "I spent the next 10 minutes trying to clean up my carpet and waiting for my hand to stop burning," you win the grand prize. Don't worry, the dog was not harmed.

I had three options:

1) Stand there berating myself for being stupid, then allow myself to head down a shame spiral about how I never do anything right, which would've ultimately screwed up my whole day and I never would've sat down to write this brilliance that you are currently reading.

2) Admit that carrying everything up at the same time might not have been the brightest decision I've made today, finish the trek up the stairs, dry off the bottom of the mug and place it next to my computer then head back down the stairs to dry the floor (and say a silent prayer to the gods of floor coverings that I don't have to figure out how to get raspberry tea stains out of cream-colored carpeting), and then move on with my day, while pledging to just make two trips in the future.

3) Do all of number two, except that I don't learn from the experience and find myself repeating my "trip saving" behavior in the future.

Now I haven't decided between option two or three yet, but I'm definitely not going to spend the day beating myself up over the mistake.

Your situation may be a tad bit more serious than spilling tea (are you allowed to cry about that? I know it's not milk, but...), but you can still apply the same reasoning and the same options.

Exercise

I want you to refer back to that list you made of times when you made a mistake or a poor choice (or start the list if you didn't do it before) and engaged in uncompassionate behavior or self-talk. We need about three examples to work with.

1) _____

2) _____

3) _____

Once you've written those down, I want you to come up with three different ways that you could have handled them.

1) a.

    b.

    c.

2) a.

    b.

    c.

3) a.

    b.

    c.

Now, this exercise isn't to get stuck in the coulda, shoulda, wouldas. It's time to flex your self-compassion muscles for the next time that you do something less than stellar.

Surviving to Thriving

Chapter 15

You Should Do Stand-up

Can we all agree on something? Humanity, life, our bodies, the things that happen to us... they are utterly ridiculous. Here we are walking around trying to hold our heads high and maintain our dignity while silly noises come out of our bodies, the universe appears to be conspiring against us, and we make the most ridiculous faces during sex. I once heard a comedian say that if you ever wanted to never have sex again... video tape it.

Even the most erudite, prudish, uptight person is still absolutely absurd behind closed doors. Now, I'm not writing this chapter to condone fart jokes, but rather to show you that life is inherently silly. If you take it (and yourself) too seriously... well, shit's not going to go down so good for you.

Ever since I was a little girl, people have told me that I should do standup. While I appreciate the compliment, and have actually done standup (terrifying!), my humor is more than just a hobby. My sense of humor is a protective mechanism that I developed early on in life. When your parents divorce at the age of three and you move in with an emotionally abusive grandparent, you better start finding the funny where you can.

My divorce was one of the most difficult experiences of my life. Luckily my ex-husband was a pedophile (How often do you hear that?), so the jokes flowed like wine.

I'm not feeling very funny.

It's interesting that some of the funniest people we know, become utter drags when their world gets a little topsy-turvy. It's like all of a sudden their funny bones have just up and left.

There are a few reasons for this.

1) They think that if they joke about a situation, they are making light of it and no longer understand the gravity of the challenge at hand.

2) They are so wrapped up in the "pain and suffering" of the experience, that they can't find anything to laugh about.

The problem is, this is when humor is the most important. Brafman talks about humor in <u>Succeeding When You Are Supposed to Fail</u>:

> Because humor protects us from the intensity of stress, it is much more than just a positive quality we normally associate with charm and wit. A highly developed sense of humor is linked to intelligence and resilience — the ability to bound back from failure or setbacks. Unfortunately, when dealing with a crisis, the first thing that is usually sacrificed is humor. We tell ourselves that this is no time for levity, the situation is too serious. In fact, it may be when we need comic relief the most.

My stepmom is an extremely funny person. She can delight audiences with tales of her early adulthood, accidentally stealing a car, lighting her backseat on fire with a tossed cigarette, chasing an intruder through the streets of Queens, naked and brandishing a butcher's knife. She's funny as shit. But she is never funnier than the night before surgery. As a family, we've seen this multiple times and her pre-surgical standup rivals that of George Carlin (moment of silence for one of the greats).

"Playful humor enhances survival for many reasons," said resiliency authority Al Siebert in <u>The Survivor Personality</u>. "Laughing reduces tension to more moderate levels." From a psychological standpoint, choosing to use humor can be empowering and productive. "Playing with a situation makes a person more powerful than sheer determination [does]," Siebert explains. "The person who toys with the situation creates an inner feeling of 'This is my plaything; I am bigger than it ... I won't let it scare me.'"

It may seem counterproductive, but making light of a dark situation actually allows you to process your emotions and come to a solution faster. If you've ever been around law enforcement or emergency medical responders, you get to see this type of comedy (often called Gallow's Humor) in action. Cops, EMTs, crime scene techs, see things that no human should ever have to see. Violence, carnage, devastation. Basically, the worst that humanity has to offer, constantly. How do they handle it? Humor. They make jokes (sick, morbid jokes) to relieve the tension and process the emotions.

The last class I took in graduate school was reviewing FBI files of violent, generally unthinkable crimes, and writing a thesis based off of them. My friend and I sat in a tiny library three days a week, reading up on all the awful things that people do to each other. I'm not allowed to go into detail because I signed something a long time ago, and I don't want to go to jail, but let's just say those files included stories of decapitation (resulting in a new Halloween decoration), produce placed into crevices that should not normally accommodate nightshades, and pictures. Tons and tons of pictures. If it hadn't been for the "What a great dish for your candy corn" and "I've never thought of putting an eggplant there" jokes, we probably wouldn't have survived.

Humor doesn't just provide psychological benefits. There is a physiological response to humor as well. When we laugh our muscles relax, breathing becomes more normal, blood pressure drops, and our ability to tolerate pain increases. Our bodies release endorphins (feel good chemicals) and our immune response increases. This last one is especially important as a constant state of stress wears on our immunity and makes it easier to succumb to illness.

Are you ready to sharpen your funny bone?

Exercise

Let's take a look at the current challenge you are facing and put a funny spin on it. In order to do this, you will need to release any judgment you may have about making light of a bad situation.

Right now _____ is very hard for me.

I can laugh at it because:
_____

_____

Let me share an example. I told you that my now ex-husband was arrested for soliciting a minor online. Suckfest of epic proportions. Here's how I found some humor:

1) He had taken a photo with his little cousins a few years earlier. He was unkempt, unshaven, wearing a ratty old t-shirt, and looking generally unsavory. I teased him for years about not letting that man anywhere near children... don't think I forgot about that picture after his crime.

2) There was a children's book series that came out around the same time called "No David, No!." Let's just say that got quoted an awful lot.

3) When I read the transcripts of his conversations with the "minor" (it was actually an undercover cop), I had a good laugh over one line. My ex said: "How would you like to have a pizza and some sex?" I found this hilarious. The pizza was terrible in North Carolina!

4) I love making the joke that my ex tried to leave me for a younger woman.

Sick? Yep. A tad morbid? Yep. Making light of a terrible crime. Yep. Helped me through one of the most difficult experiences of my life? You betcha.

Find humor in your misery and life will go a lot smoother.

Chapter 16

Poof! You Are Resilient

Phew! (wipes sweat from forehead). We've had quite the journey here, haven't we? We've laughed, we've cried, we may have squeezed the crap out of our furry family members (hopefully not literally, that would be quite messy).

As I mentioned early on in this book, not everything in here may resonate with you and not everything may apply to your individual situation. That's why I included so many different topics. There may even be certain chapters that you read and went "Duh, I'm already doing that." In which case... yay! See, I told you that you were already amazing. You just need a reminder every once in a while.

It seems to be life's greatest irony that when we need to use our coping skills the most, when we need to lean on our support systems, when we need to practice self-care and self-kindness... it's precisely when we don't.

I didn't tell you anything earth-shattering. I don't have the secrets to the universe (though I've always suspected that all of life's answers can be found in the sitcom *How I Met Your Mother*). If you are looking for divine enlightenment, I suggest that you make a trek up to visit the Dali Lama. If you are looking to handle the curve balls that life keeps throwing at you, look no further. You already have the strength, the gumption, and the balls to survive whatever you are facing. You are already a superhero, kickass, resilient person!

For every hardship you overcome, for every challenge you kick in the ass, for every life-altering experience that you harness for good, you become a better version of yourself. Embrace change, love yourself, help others, and be grateful for the amazing life you've created for yourself.

And please, whatever you do......
......stay the hell away from clowns.

Chapter 17

If At First You Don't Succeed

The funny thing about this book on resilience, is that in the first edition, I forgot to mention a really important part of overcoming setbacks. You'd think that it would've been an obvious one, but apparently I had to have a certain, awful experience before I could share my knowledge with the world.

Let me tell you how the night in question ended and then we'll backtrack into how it began.

At about 10 PM, I was sitting on the street at First Friday, clutching a service-dog-in-training for dear life. Okay, that's not out of the ordinary. Actually, that happens anytime I see a dog. What was out of the ordinary, was me standing in a crowded bar thirty minutes earlier, bawling — like a super-ugly cry — over a glass of vodka and cranberry. I was going through bar napkins like air, and neither the tears nor the snot (sorry) seemed to be stopping anytime soon.

How did that happen?

Ever since I started speaking (in front of audiences, not as a baby), I wanted to do a TED talk. Not only did I want to do one, but every time I opened my mouth in front of an audience, someone in the crowd told me I ought to do a TED talk. Unfortunately, the local TED event was no longer happening and I hadn't heard anything about a new organizer taking over.

Then one day, I was having breakfast with a new friend. Not only was TED starting up again in Las Vegas, but my friend just happened to be on the committee to select the speakers. I'd love to say that I was just jumping for joy in my head, but I'm pretty sure my butt left the chair a few times, too.

I submitted my topic: "Why Animal Rescue is Better than Anti-Depressants," and with just a few weeks until the TEDx Preview event, I received the notification that I was selected. I got to work.

I wrote my talk. I practiced my talk. There was one part that I couldn't seem to nail. Right near the beginning, I'd rattle off the side effects of anti-depressants: nausea, weight gain, fatigue, dizziness, insomnia, dry mouth, constipation, blurred vision, loss of sexual desire and even erectile dysfunction. I practiced and practiced and practiced. I was working at World Market the week before the talk and I practiced so much, my boss memorized my talk.

If you've already started to cringe, you know what's coming next. I walked into the TEDx Preview event and I was more nervous than I had ever been before. I was miked up and I headed to the front of the room. I got the first two lines out. I got the first two side effects out. And then my brain decided it was going to take a vacation. My mouth became as dry as the Sahara Desert — there may have even been a cactus in there. I watched as my friend, Kathi (who always knows the moment I forget my speech), gazed on in horror, her lips mouthing "make something up."

My mind was completely empty. Well, not completely empty. My speech was gone, but every insecurity I've ever had popped in there and started dancing around. I remember looking at the door. I remember thinking, "It's just a few feet away. Just walk off this stage and everything will be okay." But another voice popped into my head. A voice that said "If you walk off this stage, you will never step foot on another one." The crowd began to offer cheers of encouragement and I was able to gather some semblance of my talk and move forward. When the buzzer went off (I'd run out of time), I curtseyed and made a beeline for the door. Yes, I curtseyed. The sound guy stopped me right outside the door to take my mic and I managed to do the only thing that could've possibly made the situation worse.

Everyone has heard the horror story of the speaker, musician, actor, politician, etc. that forgot to take their mic off and had a conversation that wasn't meant for the whole room to hear. Apparently, that's just one of those mistakes you have to make yourself. The sound guy said, "You did great out there!" and I responded with, "Are you fricking kidding me? That fricking sucked!" (I did not say "fricking" either time).

I was too shell-shocked to even care. I just ripped the mic off my belt and ran for the green room. The text messages started coming. Was I okay? Did I need support? No. I needed a nice big rock to crawl under and hide. I needed to get out of the building before the tears started. I needed to run into traffic.

Well, I didn't get any of those. Thankfully, the mic didn't work outside of the room, but I didn't know that until my friends cornered me after to offer consolation and tell me that it wasn't as bad as I thought.

I knew in the moment, if I quit, I would never get on stage again. But it wasn't until my next speaking engagement that I realized just how difficult it would be to speak again. My mentor instructed my friends that no one was to send me a video from that talk until I'd gotten on stage again. With the TEDx disaster looming over my head, I prepared my speech for the next Unstuck Conference. I was so nervous about the conference that I brought my book on stage (the first edition of this one), just so I could have a cheat sheet with notes in case my mind decided to take another holiday.

I made it through the speech. Actually, I rocked the speech. A few days later, my mentor allowed the video to reach my hands. I was only silent for about 20 seconds. The seven-hour panic attack I had up there was only 20 seconds to the audience. In fact, a woman from the audience recognized me at First Friday a few months later. She was all excited to meet me and told me how much she enjoyed my talk. "I was so intrigued by your speech," she said. "I couldn't wait to see what you said next."

Yeah, me neither.

I'm not sure the feeling of that experience will ever go away. That, and the seasoned speakers in the room told me that it happens to everyone. In fact, it'll happen again in my career. They told me that the only thing I could do, is learn from the experience, and keep moving forward.

I guess that's what this new chapter is about. When you fall down, the only way you've actually failed, is if you never get back up. Shit happens. The only thing you can do is learn from it and move on.

Surviving to Thriving

About the Author

Sheryl Green is a storytelling expert, author, speaker, and coach. When searching for her core message and expertise, Sheryl realized just how amazing she was at getting knocked on her butt and getting back up stronger and braver than she'd ever been before. She now brings that spirit of resilience to her clients: helping individuals and businesses rewrite their stories, and live as the main character in their life's narrative.

After years of living in "comfort-zone quicksand" and a devastating divorce, Sheryl found herself in a deep depression. She hit rock bottom months later, having to be lifted up off the bathroom floor, and embarked on a journey of self discovery. Almost drowning in a sea of self-help books and seminars, Sheryl found peace in the service of others. Volunteerism, writing, and a variety of other tools allowed her to overcome her depression and find her true calling.

Sheryl is a passionate animal advocate and serves as the Director of Communications and Cuddling for Hearts Alive Village, an animal rescue in Las Vegas. Inspired by a special service dog named Pele, Sheryl founded Paw it Forward Las Vegas, an annual community event to inspire people to get involved, support animal rescue, and to be a voice for those who cannot speak.

With more than 15 years in Customer Service, six years in Mental Health and Education, and five years in the nonprofit world, Sheryl brings a unique blend of experience and insight to her clients and audiences.

Sheryl earned her Bachelor's in Psychology and Anthropology from Adelphi University in Garden City,

New York and her Master's Degree is Forensic Psychology from John Jay College of Criminal Justice in New York City. After too many years of brushing snow off her car, Sheryl now lives in Las Vegas, Nevada with her beagle/lab mix Akasha. In her spare time she likes to read, travel, hike with Akasha and do yoga (also sometimes involving Akasha).

If you'd like help writing your personal or business story, or to hire Sheryl to speak at your next event, contact Sheryl at:
sheryl@sherylgreenspeaks.com

www.sherylgreenspeaks.com

Notes

Notes

www.ingramcontent.com/pod-product-compliance
Lightning Source LLC
Chambersburg PA
CBHW052034070526
44584CB00016B/2033